I0815386

MAKING MOVIES

Essential Library
An Imprint of Abdo Publishing
abdobooks.com

BY LAURA K. MURRAY

Printed in the United States of America, North Mankato, Minnesota.
052024
092024

Cover Photos: Shutterstock Images (clapboard, light, film strip)
Interior Photos: Shutterstock Images, 1 (light), 1 (film strip), 13, 69, 101; Leonard Ortiz/Digital First Media/Orange County Register/MediaNews Group/Getty Images, 4; Robyn Beck/AFP/Getty Images, 9; Zeta Cinema/ON Cinema/Album/Alamy, 10; FG Trade/E+/Getty Images, 15; Photo12/Universal Images Group/Getty Images, 16; Donaldson Collection/Michael Ochs Collective/Getty Images, 19; Donaldson Collection/Moviepix/Getty Images, 20; Pictorial Press Ltd/Alamy, 23; LMPC/Getty Images, 27; Sally Anderson/Alamy, 28; Beth Keiser/Corbis Historical/Getty Images, 30; Gene Lester/Archive Photos/Getty Images, 37; Alex J. Berliner/ABImages/AP Images, 39; Jeff Kravitz/FilmMagic/Getty Images, 40; Warner Bros./Album/Alamy, 42, 48; Focus Features/Entertainment Pictures/Zuma Press/Alamy, 44; Rachel Luna/Getty Images Entertainment/Getty Images, 47; Niko Tavernise/7e Art/20th Century Studios/Amblin Entertainment/Photo 12/Alamy, 51; Jose Perez/Bauer-Griffin/GC Images/Getty Images, 53; Alberto E. Rodriguez/Getty Images for Disney/Getty Images Entertainment/Getty Images, 56, 65;Moviestore Collection Ltd/Alamy, 61; AaronP/Bauer-Griffin/GC Images/Getty Images, 62; Dave J. Hogan/Getty Images Entertainment/Getty Images, 66; Frazer Harrison/Getty Images for Paramount/Getty Images Entertainment/Getty Images, 70; Amanda Edwards/Getty Images Entertainment/Getty Images, 73; Joby Sessions/Tap Magazine/Future/Getty Images, 75; Sven Hoppe/dpa/picture alliance/Getty Images, 78; Plan B Entertainment/Moviestore Collection Ltd/Alamy, 82; Unique Nicole/Getty Images Entertainment/Getty Images, 85; Mandoga Media/picture alliance/Getty Images, 86; Ben Hasty/MediaNews Group/Reading Eagle/Getty Images, 88; Wesley Foulds/Shutterstock Images, 91; Giulio Benzin/Shutterstock Images, 92; Chris Pizzello/Invision/AP Images, 95; Kevin Winter/Getty Images Entertainment/Getty Images, 96; Aggapom Poomitud/Shutterstock Images, 100

Editor: Laura Stickney
Series Designer: Maggie Villaume

Library of Congress Control Number: 2023949217

Publisher's Cataloging-in-Publication Data
Names: Murray, Laura K., author.
Title: Making movies / by Laura K. Murray
Description: Minneapolis, Minnesota: Abdo Publishing, 2025 | Series: Making media | Includes online resources and index.
Identifiers: ISBN 9781098293352 (lib. bdg.) | ISBN 9798384912620 (ebook)
Subjects: LCSH: Moviemaking--Juvenile literature. | Film-making (Motion pictures)--Juvenile literature. | Production of motion pictures--Juvenile literature. | Cinematography--Juvenile literature.
Classification: DDC 791.43--dc23

CONTENTS

CHAPTER ONE

MAKING A MOVIE

Alex and Parker had finally landed on an idea for their movie: zombies! For weeks, the two teenage friends had been bouncing around ideas for their next short film. They had made other short films together and had learned a lot about filmmaking each time. The concept for their new film stemmed from a psychology paper Parker had written for school. It focused on how social media affected teens. Alex and Parker discussed possibilities for building those ideas into a film. Eventually, they came up with the idea of teens turning into zombies. They titled their film *Disconnected*.

Although Alex and Parker were making the film just for fun, they wanted it to mirror a professional production. Both teens dreamed of breaking into the film business one day. *Disconnected* was their most ambitious project yet. Alex had directed their past films, so she took the lead as the film's director and editor. Parker was a skilled writer and musician, so he would handle the script, marketing, and sound.

Some high schools and colleges offer filmmaking or film studies classes. Students learn how to use equipment such as cameras.

> **Each project comes with its own set of challenges. . . . once I feel [that a film] is important enough to make, then it is your passion, your drive, and your determination that take it to the next level.[1]**
>
> ***—Kathryn Bigelow, director***

The two friends planned to enter the movie in a virtual film festival for young filmmakers. Entrants had to upload their films directly to YouTube by the deadline. The festival's judges would view all the films and select winners in various categories, including best acting, editing, and directing. Public viewers could vote for their favorite film. The film with the most public votes would win the Audience Choice award.

To get started, Alex and Parker hashed out their story. The film would feature students who take on zombielike qualities after receiving mysterious social media messages. They wanted to explore themes of social media, isolation, and pressures that teens face. Alex wanted to pay homage to classic horror films and teen films while subverting genre expectations. Parker studied screenplays from similar movies, while Alex researched cinematography techniques.

PREPARING FOR FILMMAKING

Alex and Parker knew preparation was key to a successful production. Once their screenplay was complete, they made storyboards to visually plan each scene, shot by shot. They took stock of their resources and equipment. Alex and Parker decided to shoot the film with their smartphones, using techniques they had learned in their film class at school. Their film teacher, Mr. Colton, enthusiastically supported their interest in filmmaking. He said Alex and Parker could use school computers with the Adobe Premiere Pro video editing program.

Alex and Parker had social media accounts for their production company, A&P Productions. They posted teasers of their upcoming project, showing sneak peeks of their work. Parker shared a close-up photo of their storyboard panels. The caption read, "Exciting things in the works!" Alex and Parker also used their social media presence to reach potential cast and crew members. They would need a small number of actors and at least three crew members. Alex and Parker were thrilled when Joy, who acted in many of their school's drama productions, agreed to play the lead role.

Next, Alex and Parker chose shooting locations. After Mr. Colton signed off on the project, the school gave Alex and Parker permission to film on school property. To do so, the group had to agree to supervision, a strict time frame, and other guidelines. They acquired all necessary props and got permission to use Alex's brother's car, which would

PLANNING THE SCENE

A common term in film theory is *mise-en-scène* (pronounced "meez-on-sen"), which translates to "setting the stage." In cinema, the French phrase refers to everything in front of the camera and how it is arranged. The set, props, lighting, costumes, makeup, actor movements, and shot composition all combine to create the film's visuals. They affect what the audience sees and feels. Filmmakers consider mise-en-scène to make sure their projects accurately capture their vision.

be used in several scenes. Actors would supply their own wardrobes, but the students playing zombies would need special makeup.

Alex hadn't anticipated how challenging it would be to coordinate filming around everyone's busy schedules. The group lost two days of planned shoots due to rainy weather. Alex and Parker also needed to stay within the film's small budget. They were using money they'd earned from their summer jobs. They needed to keep expenses to a minimum, only paying extra for makeup, light rentals, and food and drinks. They allotted a small amount for marketing items, such as social media ads.

LIGHTS, CAMERA, ACTION!

As the sun set over the school's football field, Alex made sure everyone was in place. It was time to shoot the final scene of *Disconnected*. Joy waited on her mark. Parker stood nearby with a call sheet in his hand. He looked at the sheet, which listed all the actors participating in the day's shoot, as he mentally planned out the next sequence. Several of their friends held additional lights plugged into long extension cords. They stood in the designated spots Alex and Parker had tested previously to ensure that the lighting would be correct.

> **"We're in a place now where technology is so cheap that there's no excuse for you not to be making films on the weekends with your friends, shot on your iPhone.[2]"**
>
> ***—Mark Duplass, actor and director***

Small film crews must work together to prepare sets and plan shots. To stay on schedule, the crew should start acquiring props or building any necessary set pieces during preproduction.

They had limited time to shoot these climactic scenes. The school had given the group just a few days to complete filming before students returned from fall break. Earlier, the small production team had filmed scenes inside the school with students who had volunteered to act as extras.

Alex looked up at the stadium lights glowing against the darkening sky, illuminating the turf and the running track encircling the field. This was their final scene, and it was going to be one of the film's trickiest sequences. The eerie cat-and-mouse chase had to take place at night under the stadium bleachers, which posed challenges for both lighting and filming.

Alex would record from outside the bleachers to capture Joy running underneath. To film this kind of tracking shot—a moving shot that follows the subject—bigger studio productions used an expensive camera dolly moving along a track. But Alex and Parker didn't have that equipment. So Alex had rigged up a rolling flatbed cart from her parents' garage to serve the same purpose.

Alex stood on the cart with her smartphone attached to a tripod. She pressed "record" on her phone camera. After making

CLAPBOARDS

One of the most recognizable symbols in cinema is the clapboard. This is the hinged slate that filmmakers clap together when they call, "Action!" Today, the clapboard is known as a slate, the material from which original clapboards were made. Modern filmmakers use slates that are easy to write on and erase. The second assistant camera, or clapper loader, is the crew member usually responsible for the device. Clapping the slate is an important signal for the postproduction crew, marking the beginning and end of takes. Slates include the scene number, take number, and roll number, which refers to the roll of film or digital media file.

Most professional camera dollies have a seat for the camera operator and run along a track. Filmmakers can use a dolly to capture smooth shots that move toward, alongside, or away from the subject.

sure the video was recording, she yelled, “Action!” As Joy ran under the bleachers, Parker pulled the cart to keep Alex parallel with Joy. This way, Alex could keep the actress in the camera’s frame. After a few takes, they had the shot they needed. Next they filmed close-ups of Joy’s expressions and shots of another student’s shadowy form chasing her. Handheld shots would add to the scene’s chaotic, unsettling feel.

After they finished filming, Parker posted behind-the-scenes photos and video clips from the day to the A&P Productions social media accounts. “That’s a wrap!” he captioned the posts.

FINISHING TOUCHES

Over the next few weeks, Alex and Parker worked on the film’s final stages. Alex used the school’s video editing software to sort through the footage she had taken. She had uploaded and reviewed the footage after each day’s shoot but hadn’t edited it yet. She put the clips in order and selected the best takes. She adjusted the color and lighting. Meanwhile, Parker researched online sources to secure copyright-free music, some of which was in the public domain. That meant they could use it without paying someone for the rights to it. Parker also recorded original music on his guitar to use in the film.

Alex inserted the music and sound effects into the video footage. In one scene, the wind was too loud in the background, so Alex adjusted the sound levels to make

In video editing programs such as Adobe Premiere Pro, users can trim, cut, or reposition individual video clips. There are also tools for adding transitions and special effects.

00;00;08;00
00;00;16;00
00;00;24;00
00;00;32;00
Adjustment Layer
4.mp
7.mp4
5.mp4

BACK TO BASICS

Making a quality movie with a smartphone requires more than simply pointing the camera at the subject. Getting different types of shots, such as close-ups and wide shots, keeps the movie interesting for the audience. So does moving the camera position to capture various angles. Another basic tip for filmmakers is to pad the shot, which means recording extra footage before and after the action begins. That way, the filmmaker ensures they captured the full action. It also provides more material to work with while editing.

it quieter. She and Parker decided to scrap an early scene because it took attention away from the main story. Alex added titles at the beginning of the film and credits at the end. Finally, she exported the film into an mp4 file, a common video file format.

THE PREMIERE

Alex and Parker also began a marketing campaign for *Disconnected*. They created a teaser trailer and posted it on YouTube. In the trailer, they played up the movie's social media theme and mysterious plot. They used a series of taglines on their marketing materials, including "Are u still there?" and "Connection lost." Parker wrote a press release and sent it to the school newspaper. Alex created flyers and hung them at local coffee shops. Alex and Parker also asked the high school principal if they could include information about the film in the school's e-newsletter. Some of the actors even put on their zombie makeup and handed flyers to students in the cafeteria.

After a few last tweaks, Alex exported the final file of the movie. She uploaded it to YouTube and set its time and date to premiere. On premiere night, Alex and Parker gathered their friends and family, as well as the cast and crew, for a watch party on the

To share their films with others, filmmakers can host screenings or watch parties. Some people rent theaters or set up projectors for outdoor screenings. Others plan smaller events at home.

big screen at Parker's house. The YouTube live premiere featured a countdown on the screen before the film played. As the screening began, Alex and Parker watched to see the audience's reactions.

Following the film, audience members asked Alex and Parker questions about the filmmaking process. Cast and crew members shared stories about working on the film. People were already asking when A&P Productions would be starting its next project. Alex and Parker wouldn't hear back about the film festival results for a while, but seeing their vision come to life on-screen was all the fulfillment they needed. It made all their hard work worth it.

EDISON
KINETOSCOPE
EDISON
THE

CHAPTER TWO

THE HISTORY OF MOVIES

Since the late 1800s, the art of filmmaking has evolved dramatically. It has become a multibillion-dollar industry. Since the early 1900s, the US film industry has been known as Hollywood. This area in Los Angeles, California, is home to many major film studios.

In 1891, inventors Thomas Edison and William Dickson introduced the Kinetoscope. This cabinet had a window through which a person could view the illusion of a moving image. Kinetoscope parlors soon opened throughout the United States. Customers paid to view films on the machines. The films were often short clips of circus acts or sports such as boxing matches.

In 1895, Auguste and Louis Lumière patented the Cinématographe. It projected moving images for audiences. In December 1895, the Lumières held the first commercial film screening in a Parisian café's basement. The showing included their 46-second film *Workers Leaving the Lumière Factory*.[1] Audiences were astonished and delighted by short films, most of which documented scenes of everyday life.

At Kinetoscope parlors, a customer told the operator which film they wanted to see. Then the customer looked through the machine's peephole to view the film.

Moviemaking soon developed into an art form. Filmmakers such as Alice Guy-Blaché developed stories within their films and introduced special effects. In 1903, Edwin S. Porter released *The Great Train Robbery*. This 12-minute film was groundbreaking for its realistic narrative structure.[2] It became the first major box-office success.

HOLLYWOOD

Los Angeles became the central location for filmmaking in the United States. By 1915, major film studios were mainly located in Hollywood. More than 60 percent of US film production happened there.[3]

Early movies did not have sound and rarely had color. Often, music recordings accompanied movies. Later, movie theaters featured live music and orchestras. The first films were made on single reels that played for about 16 minutes. But multiple-reel films, or features, became popular by 1912.[4] Movies became longer, which meant theaters could charge theatergoers more money. Directors experimented with editing, cuts, shots, and angles, allowing audiences to engage more fully in a film's story.

Silent film stars such as Clara Bow, Charlie Chaplin, and Mary Pickford became household names. In 1927, Josephine Baker starred in *Siren of the Tropics*, becoming the first Black woman to star in a major film's lead role. This was significant because at the time, racial segregation and discrimination were widespread throughout the country.

CREATOR **SPOTLIGHT**

ALICE GUY-BLACHÉ

Alice Guy-Blaché was one of the world's first female film directors. She was born in France in 1873. She worked as a secretary for Gaumont Company, the world's first film company. Most motion pictures at the time featured documentary-style scenes. But Guy-Blaché became interested in using film to tell stories with characters, plot, and scenery.

In 1896, 23-year-old Guy-Blaché made her first film. She went on to direct, write, and supervise more than 700 films.[5] In 1910, Guy-Blaché teamed up with her husband, Herbert Blaché, and a business partner to start the Solax film company in the United States. This made Guy-Blaché the first woman to own a studio.

Guy-Blaché directed some of the first sound films and experimented with special effects. She was also one of the first filmmakers to feature diverse casts, including female heroes and all-Black casts. Her films included comedies and dramas featuring controversial topics, such as domestic abuse. Although Guy-Blaché's work influenced generations of directors, people have only recently begun to recognize her contributions. In 2018, a documentary titled *Be Natural: The Untold Story of Alice Guy-Blaché* premiered.

Alice Guy-Blaché's first film was called *La Fée aux Choux*, or *The Cabbage Fairy*. It was a whimsical story about babies growing in a cabbage patch.

Clara Bow was one of the biggest stars of the silent film era. After starring in the 1927 Paramount film *It*, Bow became known as the It Girl of the 1920s.

Cinema quickly became a key form of popular entertainment and an important US industry. Technological advancements played a huge role in the industry's growth. In 1927, Warner Bros. released the first successful movie with sound, *The Jazz Singer*. In this film, the studio took a risk on Vitaphone, a new sound technology. The film launched a new era for cinema. By 1930, most theaters showed "talkies."

Early filmmakers experimented with color, but it was not widely available until Technicolor three-color technology was introduced in the 1930s. In 1937, Walt Disney's *Snow White and the Seven Dwarfs* captivated audiences as the first fully animated motion picture featuring Technicolor. Hollywood studios later used this technology in films such as 1939's *The Wizard of Oz*.

THE STUDIO SYSTEM

The era spanning the 1920s to the 1960s is often called the Golden Age of Hollywood. During these decades, the movie industry operated under the studio system, in which a handful of studios controlled most film production and distribution. There were eight main studios, with "The Big Five" on top. These were Fox, MGM, Paramount, RKO, and Warner Bros. Along with Columbia Pictures, United Artists, and Universal Studios, these studios produced 95 percent of US movies.[6]

Under the studio system, companies kept actors, directors, and crew members under contract. They owned theater chains that played only their own films. The system allowed film companies to constantly release movies, like a factory cranking out products. The studios developed identities based on their genres and top stars. Universal became known for horror movies, while Warner Bros. became known for gangster movies and musicals.

Movies with top casts and directors were known as A-list films. A-list actors included Greta Garbo, Bette Davis, and Spencer Tracy. Many actors were bound by strict long-term contracts that

PRE-CODE HOLLYWOOD

In the film industry, the years prior to 1934 are known as Pre-Code Hollywood. This refers to the Hays Code, which was adopted in 1930 and first enforced in 1934. The Hays Code changed what material was shown on-screen. It forbade profanity, nudity, graphic violence, and material considered immoral. These rules caused controversy over censorship. The Hays Code was replaced by the modern ratings system in 1968.

gave them few rights. Some actors had no control over which roles they played. Others were forbidden from working with other studios. Actors began pushing back against the system.

The studio system had other detractors too. Some people believed established studios were so powerful that they prevented new film studios from succeeding. In 1948, the US Supreme Court agreed with this idea in the court case *United States v. Paramount Pictures*. This case broke up the Hollywood studio system, forcing studios to give up control of their theaters. The case, along with the changing economy and rise of television, marked the end of the studio system. It helped pave the way for new independent filmmakers.

Throughout the 1930s and into the 1960s, Hollywood studios developed genres that would go on to influence cinema for generations. These included science fiction, film noirs, and westerns. Orson Welles, Billy Wilder, Alfred Hitchcock, and Joseph Mankiewicz became well-known directors during this time. The Hollywood system still reflected many of the same racist and discriminatory practices as the rest of the country. However, pioneering filmmakers and actors of color, including Sidney Poitier, Hattie McDaniel, and Dorothy Dandridge, continued to make their mark. In 1964, Poitier became the first Black man to win the Academy Award for Best Actor. Throughout his career, he appeared in more than 50 films and directed nine films.[7]

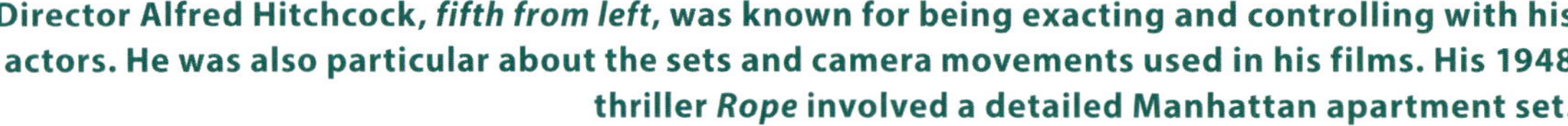

Director Alfred Hitchcock, *fifth from left*, was known for being exacting and controlling with his actors. He was also particular about the sets and camera movements used in his films. His 1948 thriller *Rope* involved a detailed Manhattan apartment set.

Sometimes we [actors] were put into solitary confinement—that was suspension—and sometimes we were let out on parole, as when we were loaned out to another studio.[8]

—Actress Olivia de Havilland, comparing the studio system to jail

CHANGING ATTITUDES

During the 1960s and 1970s, many films focused on youth culture, teenage rebellion, and rejection of social conventions. These themes echoed what was occurring in US society, as young adults rebelled against traditional values. This social upheaval was intensified by the civil rights movement and the Vietnam War (1954–1975).

The era from the mid-1960s to the 1980s is known as the Hollywood New Wave. Films of the time included *2001: A Space Odyssey* and *Easy Rider.* As attitudes shifted, films showed more sexuality and violence, as seen in *The Godfather* and *The Exorcist*. In 1968, the Motion Picture Association of America (MPAA) established the modern film rating system.

BLOCKBUSTERS AND TECHNOLOGY

The first blockbusters were released in the 1970s and 1980s. Steven Spielberg's 1975 film *Jaws* became Hollywood's first summer smash hit. It was one of the first films to be released in hundreds of theaters simultaneously. Previously, films were released to only select theaters. Seeing the success of *Jaws* and other adventure films such as

Star Wars and *Raiders of the Lost Ark*, studios began marketing movies differently. They launched massive ad campaigns and merchandise. Studios began to see the huge moneymaking potential of movies.

Film technology continued to develop throughout the late 1900s. In the 1990s, most American households owned videocassette recorders, or VCRs, which allowed them to watch films on videotape at home. This launched a new market for home videos, giving films a wider reach. Meanwhile, computer technology allowed filmmakers to introduce advanced special effects in movies such as *Jurassic Park* and *The Matrix*. In 1995, Pixar released the first fully computer-animated film, *Toy Story*. Digital video discs (DVDs) replaced videocassettes in the late 1990s and early 2000s.

BREAKING THE SILENCE

Hollywood has a long history of racism. In the silent film era, people of color were portrayed only through white people's perspective. Many were depicted with racist stereotypes. However, people of color have worked to tell their own stories in the world of film. In 1910, William D. Foster established Foster Photoplay, the first Black-owned film company. Between the late 1910s and 1940s, Black filmmakers made movies for mainly Black audiences. The films aimed to counter racist portrayals. Although many of these films were lost, organizations are working to restore them.

FROM INDIES TO DOCS

As Hollywood film budgets skyrocketed, some filmmakers took different approaches. Small-budget independent films became cult classics, including Kevin Smith's *Clerks*, Spike Lee's *Do the Right Thing*, and Joel and Ethan Coen's *Fargo*. In 1999, film students

AROUND THE GLOBE

While the US film industry grew, other countries also developed their own identities in cinema. Many influential films emerged from Japanese cinema in the 1950s. This included *Seven Samurai* and *Godzilla*. Meanwhile, French cinema highlighted movements such as surrealism in its films. India, South Korea, and the Philippines also experienced filmmaking booms during the 1950s.

created the sleeper hit *The Blair Witch Project*. Its marketing capitalized on the horror movie's fictional documentary format. The students made "missing persons" posters for the film's characters, along with a website and other online marketing materials. The movie influenced new methods of online film marketing. Meanwhile, it spawned years of imitators trying to duplicate its success.

In the early 2000s, documentary films left a lasting impression on pop culture and the public consciousness. This included Morgan Spurlock's inside look at the fast-food industry in *Super Size Me*. Another example is Michael Moore's discussion on gun violence in *Bowling for Columbine*.

FROM SUPERHEROES TO SUPERUSERS

Cinema experienced several major shifts in the 2010s. The types of movies being released were changing, and so was the way audiences watched movies. The decade was underscored with the release of superhero franchises. In 2010, *Iron Man 2* was released. The film was the sequel to 2008's *Iron Man*, which had ushered in what became the Marvel Cinematic Universe (MCU). These slick Hollywood films had budgets soaring past

$300 million.[9] Disney purchased major franchises, putting brands such as Marvel, Star Wars, and Pixar under one roof. Sequels, prequels, reboots, and remakes became more common within the film industry.

Movies used computer-generated imagery (CGI) more than ever before. This technology was used to de-age actors and create sweeping fantasy worlds. Italy's Venice Film Festival created a new virtual reality category in 2017. Filmmaking had also never been more accessible. Some filmmakers even used smartphones to create movies.

Streaming drastically changed the film landscape. In 2007, Netflix launched its streaming service. Before long, other streaming services launched, including

***Star Wars* was first released in May 1977. The space adventure film was a massive hit, eventually earning more than $775 million globally.**

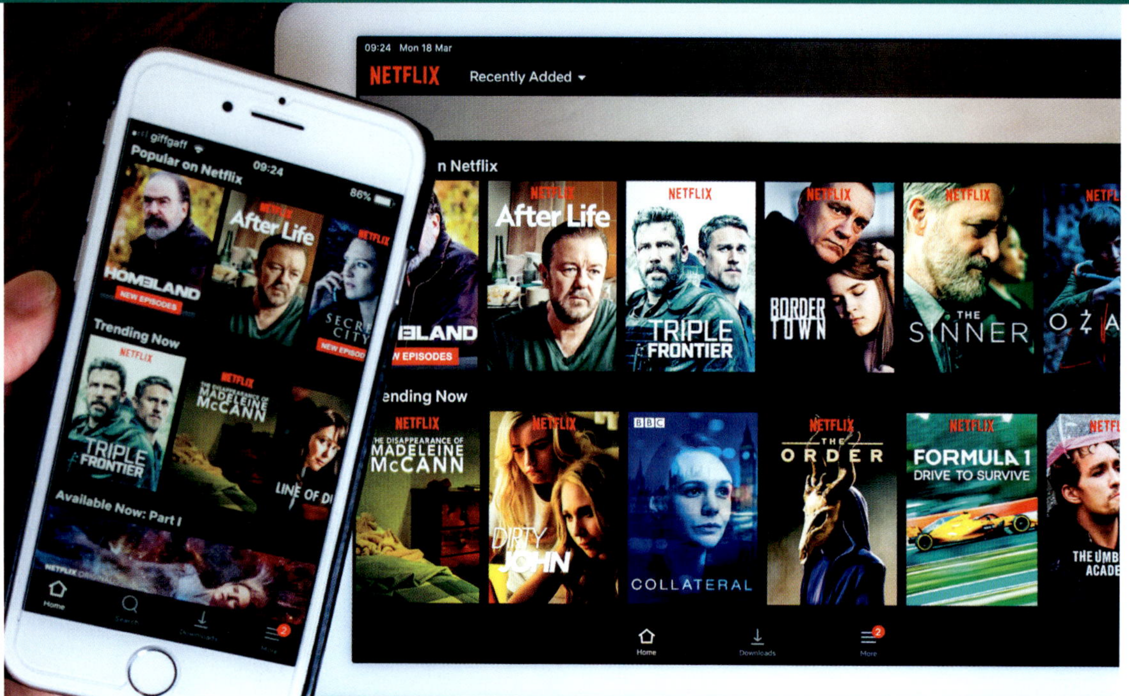

Netflix has grown into one of the leading streaming platforms, even producing its own movies. In August 2022, Netflix originals made up more than 50 percent of all titles in the platform's library.

Amazon Prime Video and Disney+. This made watching movies from home easier than ever, leading to smaller crowds at theaters.

SHIFTING ATTITUDES

In 2020, the COVID-19 pandemic brought filmmaking to a halt, forcing theaters to close. Many studios postponed releases or turned to video-on-demand (VOD) options as the pandemic continued. This opened up opportunities for indie filmmakers. With smaller production costs, they could navigate the pandemic more easily and get their films into theater spaces normally taken up by studio films. When some theaters reopened in 2021, box-office earnings were 50 percent less than they were pre-pandemic.[10] The difference in industry revenue before and after the early years of the pandemic was significant. Worldwide box-office earnings totaled $42.5 billion in 2019.[11] But they totaled only $25.9 billion in 2022.[12]

> **The good news is that with access to content and access to make content, there are lots more opportunities to tell different kinds of stories.[13]**
>
> ***—Rachel Winter, producer, 2023***

The content of movies changed too. Audiences demanded more diversity. This accompanied public reckonings over sexual abuse, pay disparities, and racism in Hollywood. Movies such as *Moonlight*, *Black Panther*, and *Everything Everywhere All at Once* featured people of color and LGBTQ+ people as protagonists. Directors Jordan Peele, Greta Gerwig, and Ava DuVernay released films. Discussions about representation continued in the early 2020s, as did debates about using artificial intelligence (AI) in films.

Today, filmmaking is more accessible than ever before. Anybody can use smartphones to make movies. People can easily distribute movies on platforms such as YouTube and Vimeo. Whether a filmmaker is creating a studio blockbuster or small-budget independent film, the basic filmmaking process applies.

INUED: (2)

73.

112

CLARK
I have to talk to you.

NE gestures at CLARK to talk.

CLARK (cont'd)
Sir... These animals... these birds...
say it.

CARMINE
What about them?

CLARK
They're endangered.

CARMINE
Not anymore. They're in Jersey;
they're fine.

CLARK
But it's against the law to bring them
into this country. It's a crime!

CARMINE
Now you're speaking in generalities...

CLARK
You assured me that my work was
legitimate.

CARMINE
't is.

CLARK
t isn't. I'm illegally transporting
ndangered species. Please, sir, I'd
ike to be let out.

CARMINE
at's an impossibility.

CLARK
ealy...

CARMINE
ave a certain standing in the
iness community, Clark. How does it
, some college boy quits on me? It's
umiliation, an infamnia. People think
something wrong with me. You understand?

Makes me look like a fool

That's

are going to

CLARK
n't tell a soul!

(CONTINUED)

PREPRODUCTION OF PROFESSIONAL MOVIES

Professional filmmaking follows an established process. The first stage is development. This involves creating a story, drafting a script, and securing funding. Development can take a few months to a few years. Writer and director James Cameron spent years developing his 1997 romantic epic *Titanic*. Other films get stuck in development. The Marvel superhero film *Deadpool* was in development for more than a decade. Beginning in 2000, various studios attempted to make the film. In 2016, 20th Century Fox finally released it.

Whether filming a professional or independent film, every filmmaker starts with the same thing: an idea. The idea may be original or based on an existing work. Many films are based on literature. For example, Alfred Hitchcock's 1960 thriller *Psycho* is based on a novel by Robert Bloch. The 2018 Netflix hit *To All the Boys I've Loved Before* is an adaption of Jenny Han's young adult book.

Some films approach existing works from a new perspective. Amy Heckerling's 1995 film *Clueless*, for example, is a modern retelling of Jane Austen's 1815

Sometimes professional movie scripts are auctioned off after a film's production. These scripts are often signed by cast members. Others belonged to specific actors and contain handwritten notes.

novel *Emma*. Other films are inspired by real people or events. Ava DuVernay's *Selma* is based on the civil rights marches of the 1960s.

STORY AND SCRIPT

Before filming begins, someone must write a script. Filmmakers may write the script themselves or hire a team of writers. Sometimes writers produce a script on spec, meaning they write it without getting paid, with the hope of later selling it to a studio. The filmmaker pitches the script to studios, producers, or investors. The goal is to get prospective clients interested in funding the film.

"Coming up with ideas is my favorite part of screenwriting. Sometimes, the ideas come just by going about my normal life and trying to be observant—and asking 'Is that a movie?'[1]"

—Justin Malen, screenwriter

Scripts written for movies or television shows are called screenplays. Screenwriters use elements such as character development and conflict. They may write in specific genres, such as science fiction or romantic comedy. Screenwriters may use various tools, such as a beat sheet that outlines the story's important moments.

Another screenwriting tool is a logline, or short summary of a film. Loglines are often just one sentence. Filmmakers use loglines at various stages of the filmmaking process, and they can be helpful when trying to sell a film.

A logline identifies the film's main characters, plot, and conflict, offering just enough information to hook the reader. The logline for *Toy Story* is, "A cowboy doll is profoundly threatened and jealous when a new spaceman action figure supplants him as top toy in a boy's room."[2]

The screenplay helps establish the film's tone. For instance, a film might be a lighthearted comedy or emotional drama. The gritty Batman film *The Dark Knight* has a much different tone than the humorous film *Guardians of the Galaxy*.

FORMATTING SCREENPLAYS

Screenplays have a standard formatting much like stage plays. Screenplay text describes the scene, action, and characters. It includes all written dialogue, with notes describing the tone of voice in which lines should be said. Screenplays may also include information about the type of shot, point of view, and transitions. Today, people use software to format screenplays.

GETTING THE DEAL

Studios or production companies may make deals with a writer to secure rights to their story. One method is optioning a story. In an option deal, the writer gets a small portion of an agreed-upon amount of money while the buyer gets exclusive rights to a story for a certain length of time.

The buyer shops the film around, trying to get production companies or studios to agree to make the movie. If the buyer is successful, the writer gets the full amount of money previously agreed upon. If time runs out, the rights to the story revert back to the writer.

Another deal is known as packaging. The story's buyer tries to get actors or directors attached to, or associated with, a project. Then they shop around the script and try to get funding, using the attachment of the actors or directors to create confidence in the project. A movie from a first-time screenwriter may not have much traction on its own. But if a studio head knows that acclaimed actress Meryl Streep is attached to the project, that would generate interest. It could increase the film's chances of moving forward.

To make a film, professional filmmakers must also have enough money to fund it. Most movies are financed through film studios. Financing can also come from other distributors, production companies, and private investors. For big-budget films, a large studio such as Warner Bros. or Paramount may invest a portion of the total production budget, while international distributors invest other funding. Some of the most expensive movies include installments of franchises. *Star Wars: The Force Awakens* had a budget of $447 million, while *Jurassic World: Fallen Kingdom* had a $432 million budget.[3]

PREPRODUCTION

Once funding is secured, a film moves into preproduction. Filmmakers finalize the budget and confirm schedules. They hire cast and crew members and lay out all details for shooting. The filmmaker also assembles a creative team. The director is one of the first people brought onboard. Directors oversee all aspects of a film, but they usually don't have complete control over creative decisions. Instead, the studio and producer have the final say.

A key part of preproduction is breaking down the script. This means the script is put into a standard format. The assistant director often does this, dividing the screenplay into scenes and listing all actors and props involved. The script breakdown also notes whether scenes take place at night or during the day, along with whether they include exterior or interior shots.

Another step is making a shot list. This pre-filming checklist includes every shot that will be in the movie, including details such as camera movements. Directors may use storyboards, or visual representations of scenes. They include drawings of every shot, similar to how panels in a comic book tell a story. Another tool is a floorplan, in which a scene's overhead view is drawn out to show the placement of the cast, set pieces, and cameras.

Storyboards and floorplans are useful in many aspects of filmmaking. Having a visual format assists the director in planning scenes. It also helps production designers create the set and choreographers set up dances or fight scenes. Storyboards help the cast and crew understand each shot.

PROTECTING WORK

Writers often register their scripts with organizations such as the Writers Guild of America (WGA). Writers can register scripts, lyrics, and other works on the WGA website. While doing so doesn't copyright the work, it officially documents the date on which the work was written. This registration can be used as legal evidence if someone else uses the work without permission.

CAST AND CREW

Today, most Hollywood movies require teams of hundreds of people. A film's budget and special effects affect the number of employees. A big blockbuster may have thousands of credited crew members. For instance, 2013's *Iron Man 3* has more than 3,700 names and 24 special-effects companies listed on its Internet Movie Database (IMDb) web page.[4]

Filmmakers assemble their department heads during preproduction. They include assistant directors, the director of photography (or cinematographer), production managers, and costume designers. The rest of the crew is also hired at this stage. This includes the departments of casting, camera and lighting, sound, art, hair and makeup, stunts, and special effects. Medics, office assistants, caterers, and accountants may also be needed.

During preproduction, the casting director chooses actors for the film. For studio films, the casting director is usually assisted by a team. The process involves auditions and screen tests, in which actors are filmed. Sometimes prospective actors receive callbacks, or requests for follow-up auditions. Casting directors may also have actors do chemistry tests, in which actors perform

EARLY SUPPORTERS

Today, studios occasionally purchase scripts or stories before they are published. In 2010, Margot Lee Shetterly began writing a nonfiction book about Black female mathematicians at NASA. In 2014, she was still working on the final draft when she sold the film rights to publishing company William Morrow. The publishers found a production company to make the film. The movie based on Shetterly's book, *Hidden Figures*, was released in 2016.

In the 1930s, filmmakers at Walt Disney Studios were the first to use film storyboards. Storyboarding helped them plan and visualize scenes in animated movies such as 1959's *Sleeping Beauty*.

MUSICAL
INTRODUCTION

together on-screen. The casting team analyzes how the actors work together on camera and decides whether they fit the roles.

Sometimes well-known actors are offered a role in a film without having to audition. This may happen if an actor has done impressive work or if filmmakers think the actor will attract audiences to the film. However, being a big Hollywood star doesn't guarantee a role, especially when the role has generated significant interest.

LOCATIONS AND SCHEDULES

Scheduling is another key part of preproduction. The number of shooting days, people, and pieces of equipment all affect a film's budget. Sometimes filmmakers adjust their plans to align with their budget. If film planning is coming in over budget, filmmakers often try to cut down the number of filming locations. They may reduce how many actors are in a scene. For example, due to a limited budget, much of Quentin Tarantino's 1992 film *Reservoir Dogs* takes place in a warehouse.

Filmmakers may also create a DOOD report, which stands for "day out of days." This document helps schedule and track the cast's workdays. It tracks things such as

> **"I was always asking questions about what do we want to say, what does this mean, how can we further enhance what we want to say in the story. I've always worked in my mind's eye.[5]"**
>
> ***—Ellen Kuras, cinematographer and director***

Renowned costume designer Colleen Atwood has created costumes for dozens of films. In 2017, she won the Academy Award for Best Costume Design for her work on the film *Fantastic Beasts and Where to Find Them*.

CREATOR **SPOTLIGHT**

RUTH E. CARTER

Ruth E. Carter has designed costumes for many films. In 2019, she became the first Black person to win the Academy Award for Best Costume Design. She won for her work in the superhero film *Black Panther*. For the film, Carter created designs based on Afrofuturism, a concept that explores Black identity, history, and culture through sci-fi and fantasy elements. Carter's designs were inspired by traditional African clothing, including that of the Maasai and Ndebele people. After researching different African cultures and traveling to South Africa, Carter received permission to use traditional designs in the film. This added an important element to the film's characters.

Before moving to Hollywood, Carter worked for costume departments in her Massachusetts hometown and the Santa Fe Opera. She broke into the movie industry after designing costumes for director Spike Lee's 1988 film *School Daze*. She worked with Lee and other major directors throughout her career.

Carter received an Academy Award nomination for her work on Lee's 1992 film *Malcolm X*. She was also nominated for her work on Steven Spielberg's 1997 film *Amistad* and Ryan Coogler's 2022 film *Black Panther*: *Wakanda Forever*.

In 2023, Ruth E. Carter became the first Black woman to win two Academy Awards. She won for her costume designs in *Black Panther: Wakanda Forever*.

an actor's first day of work, if the actor is working or traveling, or if the actor is on call. Tracking each actor's schedule keeps the production process efficient and helps filmmakers stick to their budget.

It is also important because many professional actors are part of unions. These groups aim to improve working conditions within their industry. The two main US film unions are the Actors' Equity Association and the Screen Actors Guild–American Federation of Television and Radio Artists (SAG-AFTRA). Being part of a union helps people in the film industry negotiate contracts, protect their rights, and ensure fair pay for their work. Some actors have terms about their working conditions, and violating those terms could jeopardize a production.

During preproduction, filmmakers secure all rentals and permits. Locations can make or break a film's story and budget. Some scenes are filmed on soundstages or back lots. Location scouts find filming locations for other scenes, gaining permission to shoot there. Some states or countries offer tax incentives to encourage filmmakers to work there.

Meanwhile, the costume department prepares wardrobe pieces and does fittings to make sure costumes fit the actors. The production design department builds sets and models. The cast rehearses and does read-throughs of the screenplay. Some actors train for roles, learning choreography or stunts. Natalie Portman learned ballet for the 2010 thriller *Black Swan*, while Margot Robbie learned to ice skate for the 2017 film *I, Tonya*.

PRODUCTION OF PROFESSIONAL MOVIES

After preproduction, the production stage begins. At this point, all elements of the film are ready, including props, permits, and costumes. The main phase of shooting is called principal photography. Its goal is to capture all the footage needed to make the film.

This phase marks a critical point for a film's investors. This is because once cameras start rolling, most filmmaking costs are locked in. With so many people involved, principal photography is generally the most expensive part of filmmaking. Filmmakers must follow all planning done in preproduction to ensure the film stays on schedule and budget. The principal photography of a professional feature film usually takes one to three months.[1]

Most films require additional types of shooting that are separate from principal photography. B-roll is supplemental footage that supports the main action. This may be shot at the same time as principal photography. B-roll helps establish a film's tone, characters, or settings. The 1989 romantic comedy *When Harry Met Sally*

To film the car scenes in *Barbie*, filmmakers used blue screens, miniatures, and painted backdrops. They also used a professional camera rig to focus shots on actors Margot Robbie and Ryan Gosling.

Directors guide actors in between takes, working with them to adjust specific scenes or lines. Director Wes Anderson, *left*, worked with actors Jason Schwartzman, *center*, and Tom Hanks, *right*, on the set of the 2023 film *Asteroid City*.

includes B-roll shots of New York City throughout different seasons. This creates the sense of time passing as the story unfolds. Films may also use stock footage for this purpose. Sometimes shots with visual effects are filmed separately too.

READY TO ROLL

Before a film shoot, the cast and crew receive a call sheet. This document includes details about the shooting location and each person's call time, or the time they need to be on set. Generally, the first assistant director or production coordinator sets call times based on information from the producers and director. The department heads estimate how long each shot will take to set up and shoot.

Crew members often arrive on set earlier than the cast to prepare equipment. Camera operators set up cameras, while the lighting department sets up lighting equipment. The sound crew sets up microphones and other recording devices. Set designers prepare the set, while the prop master ensures the day's props are ready. The costume, hair, and makeup departments prepare for when the actors arrive so they can help them get ready for their scenes.

During the first part of a principal photography shoot, directors block a scene. They work out the actors' positioning, movements, and body language in relation to the camera. For professional films, many directors use stand-ins to substitute for the main actors until they figure out the blocking. The crew runs test shots to ensure that the lighting, sound, and cameras are set up the way the director wants. The actors and crew members often rehearse scenes while the cameras are running. Then the directors make adjustments before finally shooting the scene.

PRODUCTION DESIGN

Production design is a vital part of bringing a film to life. Production designers create the look of the film, ensuring that its theme and mood stay true to the vision and story. The set design department is part of the production design team. It includes the set decorator, who develops the look of the set, and the set dresser, who arranges items on the set.

SHOOTING THE FILM

During principal photography, the crew films all the shots on their shot list. This list includes the shot sizes, which relate to how much is shown within the camera frame. These range from extreme close-ups to wide shots. Directors and cinematographers use a variety of shots to help build a film's story. For example, filmmakers often use a wide shot called an establishing shot to show a scene's location. Medium shots from the waist up show a character's expressions and interactions. Close-ups capture the character's emotions. Editors often decide which shots to use during postproduction.

Multiple takes may be required while filming a scene. This may depend on the director's style and preferred methods. Director Ridley Scott, whose films include *Alien*, *Thelma & Louise*, and *Black Hawk Down*, doesn't usually focus on getting extra shots. But David Fincher, director of *Fight Club*, *The Social Network*, and *Gone Girl*, is known for getting dozens of takes.

The director, cinematographer, and producer review the day's footage, which is known as the dailies. In the past, when movies were made using analog cameras, filmmakers developed footage overnight and viewed it the next day. But with modern digital cameras, filmmakers can view footage immediately after they shoot a scene. After viewing the dailies, the film team decides if everything looks right or if they need to reshoot any scenes.

ROGER DEAKINS

Roger Deakins is one of the world's best-known cinematographers. He has worked on more than ten films with filmmakers Joel and Ethan Coen, including the 1996 cult classic *Fargo* and the 2000 film *O Brother, Where Art Thou?*[2] Throughout his career, Deakins has worked on many other acclaimed films, such as *The Shawshank Redemption* and *A Beautiful Mind*. He won the Academy Award for Best Cinematography twice, once for *Blade Runner 2049* and once for *1917*. Deakins has been nominated for the award more than 15 times.[3]

Born in England, Deakins began his career in graphic design and photography before moving into film. His first films were documentaries made in the 1970s and 1980s. Deakins is known for his masterful, creative use of cameras and light.

When shooting a scene that requires soft lighting, he may drape areas of the set with muslin cloth and arrange lights, cameras, and reflections so that the lighting is warm and soft on the actors. Deakins takes inspiration from many places. When creating the dystopian, orange-hued world of Las Vegas in *Blade Runner 2049*, Deakins was inspired by images of a dust storm in Australia.

For the 2019 war drama *1917*, Roger Deakins worked to make the film appear as if it were shot in just one seamless take.

CHOREOGRAPHY, SPECIAL EFFECTS, AND STUNTS

Days on set look different for different movies, requiring various types of preparation, blocking, and rehearsals. Damien Chazelle's 2016 film *La La Land* involved choreographed musical dance numbers that included dozens of dancers. The film's dazzling opening dance number, which is set on a freeway during a traffic jam, featured 30 professional dancers and more than 100 extras. The scene, which clocked in at just under four minutes, took 47 takes.[4]

Choreography also comes into play for fight scenes. Ang Lee's film *Crouching Tiger, Hidden Dragon* is known for its sleek martial arts scenes, which feature swordplay and flying fighters in ballet-like sequences. During production, perfecting these choreographed battle scenes took 80 of the movie's 100 total shoot days.[5] Other action movies, such as the *Mission: Impossible* franchise, require carefully planned stunts performed by professionals. This may require hiring stunt doubles who can stand in for actors, along with acquiring safety equipment such as harnesses.

During principal photography, some movies employ special effects, or SFX. The team may create practical

> **Film is so collaborative; you really have to understand other people's jobs.[6]**
>
> ***—Dean Cundey, director of photography***

Directors may review footage in between takes. Some directors, such as Greta Gerwig, watch footage alongside the actors involved in a scene.

special effects without CGI. This may involve makeup, prosthetics, masks, sculptures, mechanical devices, and puppets. The 1993 film *Jurassic Park* made pioneering use of CGI. But its filmmakers also used practical special effects to create the film's dinosaurs. They relied on puppetry, animatronics, and costumes. Movies may also use visual effects, or VFX. These are often created digitally during postproduction editing. For example, actors may shoot scenes in front of a green screen. In postproduction, editors can then replace the green backdrop with different backgrounds and effects.

Although modern CGI technology has changed how movies are made, many films still utilize practical effects. *Top Gun: Maverick* was one of 2022's most successful movies. Its filmmakers aimed to keep visual effects discreet. First, they shot the aerial action sequences, putting cameras inside plane cockpits while the actors were in flight. The actors rode in planes piloted by professionals. They also shot some scenes on a set, with the actors inside a rotating cockpit. Later, filmmakers added computer-generated effects, such as explosions, to these live-action shots after principal photography was completed.

POSTPRODUCTION

Once principal photography ends, the movie enters postproduction. This process involves a big team. First, filmmakers transfer their footage to a reliable storage site so the film files are secure. The editor reviews the raw footage, choosing and assembling the clips

Movie musicals often involve large, complex dance numbers. For the 2021 remake of *West Side Story*, choreographer Justin Peck worked with cast members to film dances on New York City streets.

to build the narrative. This requires sifting through many takes and shots. Editing can have a huge impact on how a film's story unfolds. For example, the iconic shower scene in Alfred Hitchcock's 1960 horror film *Psycho* owes its fame to postproduction editing. The scene's quick cuts and screeching violin sounds were added during this stage.

MEMORABLE STUNTS

Movie stunts performed by professionals stand the test of time. In the 1923 silent film *Three Ages*, comedian and stuntman Buster Keaton leaps from building to building with only nets in place below. Nearly a century later, 2011's *Mission: Impossible–Ghost Protocol* featured another famous building stunt. Actor Tom Cruise scales and then rappels down Dubai's Burj Khalifa, the world's tallest building. The film team meticulously planned the stunt to make sure nothing went wrong. They spent a month setting up the shot.[7]

Edits and cuts establish the pace of the story to keep audiences engaged. Transitions between clips are important too. Scenes that jump from one shot to another without reason can be distracting. Another basic editing technique is color correction, which involves adjusting brightness, contrast, and saturation. All shots in the film should look like they belong in the same movie. If one clip's colors are deeply saturated and another's are muted, the editors must adjust the color levels accordingly.

Once the film is edited, the VFX team adds visual effects or CGI. The cinematographer makes sure the overall look reflects the vision of the film. Next, the sound department works on all the sound in the film, including dialogue and sound effects. These crew members take out unwanted noises and add background noises, voiceovers, music, and sound effects. Crew members

Many professional filmmakers use digital clapboards to mark the beginning and end of takes. This helps the editor know how to align scenes and sounds in the footage.

COLOR OF FILM

Filmmakers use color to enhance a movie's tone, story, and characters. They also use color to elicit reactions from the audience. This is known as color theory. Director Wes Anderson uses distinct color palettes to visually tell the stories of his films. For example, in Anderson's film *The Grand Budapest Hotel*, vibrant colors fade or turn to black and white as the story follows the history of a once-grand hotel. In Patty Jenkins's *Wonder Woman*, color is used to show the differences between Wonder Woman's peaceful homeland and the war-torn human world. Wonder Woman's homeland is shown in bright, warm colors, while the human world is shown in muted, desaturated colors.

called Foley artists are responsible for creating sound effects, such as doors creaking or waves crashing.

Most professional films have scores created by a composer. If filmmakers want to put existing music in the movie, the music supervisor must secure the rights to use it. Sound mixers ensure the audio levels of dialogue, sound effects, and music are balanced. Depending on the film, postproduction may take a few months or more than a year.

GETTING IT RIGHT

Additional filming may be needed after principal photography wraps. Occasionally, scenes must be rescheduled due to issues such as weather. Other times, reshoots may be needed because of technical issues. Filmmakers often shoot additional scenes after principal photography to help clarify the story. These are called pickups.

Sometimes scenes have poor sound quality that can't be fixed in postproduction. An actor's lines may be muffled or interrupted by on-set noises, such as a dog barking in the distance. When this happens, actors rerecord their lines in a studio. This is called automated dialogue replacement (ADR).

The *Lord of the Rings* film trilogy included ADR because some scenes were shot near an airport. The filmmakers decided it would be less expensive to use ADR rather than wait for planes to pass by the shooting locations. Filmmakers may also decide to make changes to the story that require actors to rerecord their lines using ADR.

One of the final elements of postproduction is adding the titles and credits to the film. The editor usually does this task. Once everything is ready, the editor exports the digital file of the finished film so it's ready for audiences to view. Another editing team works on creating movie trailers. These previews are generally about two minutes long. They aim to get audiences excited about the film.

"Everything funnels back to the editor, because the editor is going to hit the final export and send it. It's up to that editor in postproduction to explore the web that's created and bring everything to the center—whether it's motion design, retouching, sound mixing, color grading, or music.[8]"

—Cody Liesinger, video editor

MARVEL STUDIOS
AVENGERS
ENDGAME
WORLD PREMIERE

CHAPTER **FIVE**

DISTRIBUTION OF PROFESSIONAL MOVIES

Once a film is ready to share with audiences, the next step is distribution. Distributors license films and market them to ensure they make as much money as possible. Distributors also deliver films to theaters for viewing. Distribution may be through theatrical release, or playing the film in movie theaters. It may also be through VOD streaming, DVD sales, or TV broadcasting.

A movie's financial success relies on its distribution. If a movie never gets distributed—or is not distributed well—it cannot earn back its costs and make a profit. Large studios often have their own distribution companies, while independent filmmakers may market their films to distribution companies.

Filmmakers sign contracts with film distributors. These include information such as the term length, or how long the distributor has rights to the film. For studio films, this period often ranges from 10 to 15 years.[1] The agreements also specify how the film's earnings will be divided. Professional filmmakers often work out distribution deals far in advance, usually during a film's development stage.

Professional movies with theatrical releases may have large premiere events, during which the film is screened for the first time. Cast and crew members often attend these screenings.

RESEARCHING THE AUDIENCE

Throughout production, a film studio may survey audiences for their reactions to titles, trailers, and marketing material. Once a studio has a rough cut of a film, it may show test screenings to audiences of several hundred people. The company may also gather smaller focus groups to view and discuss the film. Some studios choose not to hold test screenings. They may want to keep the film secret or prevent spoilers. Sometimes responses from test screenings prompt filmmakers to make changes to a film. John Hughes's 1986 romantic comedy *Pretty in Pink* famously changed the love interest whom Molly Ringwald's character ends up with after test audiences booed the original ending.

Producers and distributors may make various types of agreements. Sometimes the distributor pays the producer a flat fee for the rights to distribute the film. This is called a leasing model. In a profit-sharing model agreement, the parties agree to receive a percentage of the film's box-office earnings. Generally, film distributors receive 10 to 50 percent of the profits.[2] Many distribution contracts are a mix of these two models. The distributor may pay the filmmaker an advance payment for the film, which can help with production expenses. Then the parties share the profits after the film's release.

Studio films usually have a theatrical release. In general, major studios want to have their movies debut exclusively in theaters because they make more money that way. Often, distributors wait to release a film on DVD or VOD, hoping to first maximize revenue from the film's theatrical showings.

But today, the growth of streaming services is changing cinemas. Fewer people go to movie theaters. Because of this, many studios are coming up with plans to release their films through streaming services soon after their theatrical releases.

Some streaming services, such as Netflix, even release their own films. Edward Berger's 2022 film *All Quiet on the Western Front* was nominated for nine Academy Awards, including Best Picture.[3] But it was not released in theaters. After premiering at the Toronto International Film Festival, the film was distributed by Netflix and released directly to streaming.

MARKETING THE FILM

The distributor is also responsible for marketing the film. The goal is to have the film shown in as many places as possible. Some companies only distribute films locally, so the film's producers may work with several different local distributors to get the film shown in multiple places.

There are many ways to market a movie and attract attention for it. Studio films use lots of marketing avenues. They may pay for TV commercials and magazine ads. They may use the internet to attract people to the movie's website or social media pages, where they can find previews and information about the film. The film's director and actors may go on promotional tours, doing interviews

> **"We are in show *business*. To be a successful business, you need an audience and you need to find the best ways to reach your target audience. . . . The first impression counts![4]"**
>
> ***—Alida Pantone, director of London's Rolling Film Festival***

> **We gave people little elements of the movie to stimulate curiosity and that created conversation. . . . Then it did totally take on a life of its own.**[6]
>
> ***—Josh Goldstine, Warner Bros. president of global marketing, on* Barbie**

on TV, on the radio, or online. Film trailers and previews may also be shown at movie theaters.

The marketing team often comes up with taglines for a film. These are short slogans or catchphrases, many of which include clever phrases or puns about the film's plot. One example is the 2010 film *The Social Network*, which tells the story of Facebook. Its tagline was "You don't get to 500 million friends without making a few enemies." Other taglines reference the viewer's experience. The 1975 film *Jaws*, which features a great white shark terrorizing swimmers, had the tagline "You'll never go in the water again."[5]

BUDGETS AND PARTNERSHIPS

A film's budget dictates the scope and target of the film's marketing. A big studio film will likely have the budget to run television ads or put up a huge billboard in New York City's Times Square. The marketing budget of Greta Gerwig's 2023 film *Barbie*, distributed through Warner Bros., was estimated to be $150 million. This was larger than the film's $145 million production budget. In what *Variety* magazine called "the marketing campaign of the year," the *Barbie* marketing team meticulously planned out a strategy to create buzz for the movie even while filming was still in progress.[7] During production, the team released an image of Barbie driving her Corvette. This sparked interest that exploded across the internet.

Barbie's marketing team had a licensing deal with Mattel, the maker of the doll. The team also had partnerships with other big brands, including Xbox and Neiman Marcus. Through a partnership with Airbnb, the *Barbie* marketing team promoted a Barbie Dreamhouse mansion in Malibu, California. When the movie came out, it was a huge smash. It earned $1 billion at the global box office less than a month after its release, making it Warner Bros.' biggest hit to date.[8] In the process, Greta Gerwig became the first solo female director to helm a billion-dollar movie.

A film's marketing team often creates eye-catching visuals for promotional materials. The poster for Wes Anderson's *The Grand Budapest Hotel* featured a quirky, distinctive image of a pink building where the story is set.

Billboards for the *Barbie* movie featured the tagline "She's everything. He's just Ken." The film's marketing team also set up a website where people could create their own Barbie posters.

Another aspect of film marketing is releasing different types of merchandise for the movie. This may include comic books, clothing, and toys. The merchandise of popular franchises can bring in tremendous amounts of money.

One good example is the *Star Wars* franchise. In 1977, 20th Century Fox did not believe the first *Star Wars* movie would be successful. So director George Lucas gave up a $500,000 payment from the company in order to keep the rights to licensing and merchandise for the franchise. The decision paid off. Since then, the *Star Wars* franchise has earned around $32 billion through merchandise alone.[9] Other film franchises with successful merchandise campaigns include *Frozen*, *Cars*, *Harry Potter*, and *Transformers*.

WORKING WITH THE MEDIA

An important part of film marketing is working with the media. The film distributor often contracts with a public relations (PR) company. Publicists are part of these companies. A film's publicist creates a press release. This document is generally one to two pages long and explains basic information about the movie. The information is often framed in a way that makes journalists or media outlets want to cover it.

Sometimes a film has an electronic press kit (EPK), a promotional tool used by musicians, filmmakers, and other artists. An EPK is a collection of digital materials that gives viewers an idea of a film's story and makes them want to learn more. A film's EPK may include trailers, clips, behind-the-scenes footage, and interviews with cast and crew members. An EPK makes it easy for media outlets to share news about the film, such as when an actor will appear on talk shows to discuss it. Oftentimes, talk shows share film clips from the EPK.

PRESS JUNKET

To promote a movie, a studio film's publicity team may invite media outlets to a press junket. This is a daylong event in which the film's director, main cast, and crew members participate in back-to-back media interviews. They aim to fit in as many interviews as possible in a short amount of time. Press junkets may feature large-group interviews along with one-on-one interviews.

DELIVERING THE FILM

Traditionally, distributors physically delivered film reels to movie theaters. Today, film delivery involves sending the film as a Digital

Cinema Package (DCP). The high-resolution files are encrypted, or protected from unauthorized use, and then sent to theaters. A theater can choose to continue running a movie for a few weeks or months, depending on the film's popularity and what other movies are showing.

The growth of VOD streaming services has affected the theatrical releases of films. The time between a film's theatrical release and its arrival on VOD has shrunk in recent years. It was especially affected in 2020, when the COVID-19 pandemic shut down movie theaters. In some cases, studio films even become available on streaming services while they are still being shown in theaters.

Theatrical distribution has continued to recover since the pandemic. In 2022, Matt Reeves's *The Batman* was the first Warner Bros. movie in more than a year to be released exclusively in theaters. The previous year, Warner Bros. released all its films through the HBO Max streaming service on the same day as the theatrical release. This method of releasing a movie on multiple platforms at the same time is known as a day-and-date release.

RELEASING A MEGAHIT

The most successful debut at the box office was the 2019 film *Avengers: Endgame*, released by Walt Disney Studios Motion Pictures. The star-studded superhero movie brought in $357 million during its opening weekend. It grossed a total of $858 million in 4,662 US theaters. Its worldwide gross totaled $2.79 billion, making it the highest-grossing film ever at the time.[10] Disney spent more than $200 million on marketing alone, including a Super Bowl commercial, multiple trailers, and publicity tours. It also had promotional partnerships with Google, Audi, Coca-Cola, McDonald's, Geico, and Ulta.[11]

Cast and crew members may promote their films at conventions or other events. The cast of *Blank Panther*, for example, attended the 2016 San Diego Comic-Con.

Film studios and distributors continue to revise their models in the industry's changing landscape. According to the website IndieWire, the average length of time that a film plays in theaters before home release is about 35 days. But there is no set standard for when a movie will become available for at-home viewing. In 2023, Universal was the only major studio that followed a consistent pattern for its theater release schedule. Its movies were exclusively in theaters for three weeks before moving to VOD or streaming services. However, if a movie earned more than $50 million in its opening weekend, it stayed exclusive to theaters for five weeks.[12]

CHAPTER **SIX**

DEVELOPING AND PRODUCING INDEPENDENT MOVIES

Independent films, or indies, are movies made without funding by major film studios or production companies. People make independent films for many reasons, including limited budgets. First-time filmmakers, actors, and crew members often get their starts in independent movies. However, just because a film is independent does not mean it is lower in quality than a studio film.

Many filmmakers choose to make indie films because they prefer working outside the Hollywood system. Working on an indie film gives them more creative control to execute their vision. For many indie filmmakers, the goal is not to create a box-office blockbuster. But some indie films still achieve commercial success.

Indie films follow the same general filmmaking process as big studio films. The project starts with development and then moves into preproduction and production. Then comes postproduction and distribution. But unlike major studio films, indie films typically have smaller budgets and involve fewer people. Big studio films have many departments with specific responsibilities, including

Elliott Hasler, *right*, founded his own indie film production company, Relsah Films. He directed the 2022 film *Vindication Swim*, which tells the story of the first British woman to swim the English Channel.

screenwriters, production managers, and the first assistant director. But indie filmmakers may fulfill some or all of those duties themselves. To stay organized, filmmakers may use project management tools, such as the StudioBinder filmmaking software.

PASSION PROJECTS

Even big stars may have to get creative to find financial backing for their projects. In the early 2000s, Hollywood star George Clooney was one of the industry's highest-paid actors. In 2005, Clooney directed and starred in the historical drama film *Good Night, and Good Luck*, which he cowrote with Grant Heslov. Clooney was passionate about the project and funded much of it himself, even mortgaging his house to do so. He paid himself just three dollars for writing, acting, and directing. He also secured investors to serve as executive producers on the film, which eventually earned more than $54 million on a $7 million budget.[1]

GETTING STARTED

As with any movie, an indie film starts with an idea that must be made into a script. First, the screenplay, schedule, and budget are created. Financing is a big consideration for any filmmaker, and it can play a role in developing the story itself.

Without the financial backing of a major studio, independent filmmakers must carefully consider their film's story and what will make it believable. For example, an independent filmmaker wouldn't plan to make a big-budget superhero movie with extensive special effects and filming locations. It wouldn't be possible with their limited budget, crew, and resources. Independent filmmakers must be prepared to cover the costs of insurance, permits, licensing, cast and crew, equipment, rentals, editing software, or contest entry fees.

Like studio films, indie films have a wide range of budgets. The 2007 horror film *Paranormal Activity*, which focuses on a family haunted by a supernatural entity, had a budget of about $15,000. It became a sleeper hit, earning $194 million.[2] The comedy-drama *Juno*, which follows the story of a teen's unplanned pregnancy, had a $6.5 million budget. It earned $232 million at the box office.[3] The 2008 British film *Slumdog Millionaire* is an indie film that had a relatively large budget of $15 million. It won eight Academy Awards, including Best Picture, and earned more than $378 million.[4]

Independent filmmakers find funding from various sources. Many contribute funding personally or ask their friends and families to help. They may get financial

Since directing *Paranormal Activity*, Oren Peli has worked as a writer, director, and producer for several of the film's sequels. He has also appeared multiple times at the Screamfest Horror Film Festival.

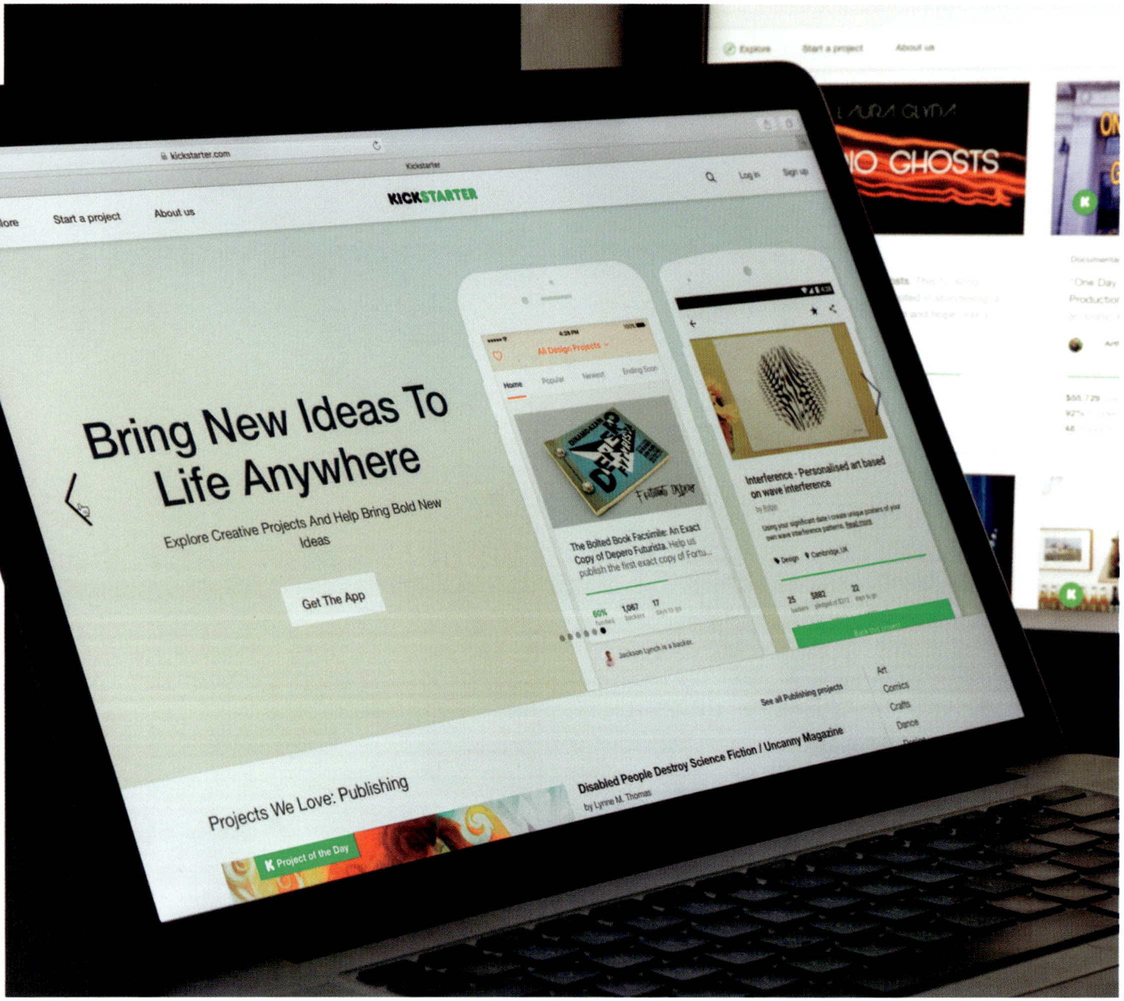

Hundreds of films funded through Kickstarter campaigns have had theatrical releases, and several have been nominated for major awards.

producers or indie film studios involved. Others apply for grants, or funding from organizations. In recent years, some filmmakers have used crowdfunding websites to raise money for their movies. Crowdfunding involves raising money through donations from a large group of people, often through the internet. Many people use websites such as Kickstarter to crowdfund creative projects.

Some crowdfunded films have gone on to achieve critical acclaim. The first crowdfunded film to win an Academy Award was *Inocente*, a 2012 coming-of-age story about an undocumented teenage girl. The film raised more than $52,000 on Kickstarter.[5] It won the Academy Award for Best Documentary Short.

SMALL BUDGETS, BIG RESULTS

In 1994, Kevin Smith released his black-and-white indie comedy *Clerks*. The premise was simple: the film followed a day in the life of store clerks. At the time, Smith was working at a convenience store. After coming up with the idea for the film, he rented a camera and got permission to shoot at the store after it closed.

KEEPING IT MINIMAL

Sofia Coppola's 2003 film *Lost in Translation* found success with a modest $4 million budget. During the 27-day film shoot, Coppola's minimal script allowed the actors, including Bill Murray and Scarlett Johansson, to improvise. The film kept production costs low by requiring little equipment and a small crew. The team also filmed at various public locations throughout Japan. For one scene, the crew shot the action from an upstairs window in a Starbucks store. Coppola worked out a distribution deal with Focus Features, and the film was released in theaters after premiering at the Telluride Film Festival. The film was a commercial success. It earned four Academy Award nominations and won the award for Best Screenplay.[6]

> **Everyone laughed loud and long at all the right times. Lines were lost in the laughter. It felt great. It felt that even if we never got picked up, the $27,000 was worth it alone.[8]**
>
> ***—Kevin Smith, on the first screening of* Clerks *in 1994***

The film budget was $27,575 in 1993, which is equal to about $57,409 in 2023.[7]

To finance the movie, Smith sold his comic book collection, borrowed money from friends and family, and maxed out credit cards. He also had family and friends play several roles in the film. Smith has since remarked that modern digital technology would have further decreased the film's cost, since camera film and equipment ate up most of the budget. *Clerks* played at the Sundance Film Festival, catapulting it into the spotlight and earning a distribution deal with Miramax. The film went on to become a cult classic and a milestone in independent, low-budget moviemaking.

Paranormal Activity was written, directed, edited, and co-produced by Oren Peli. He had never made a movie before but had considered making a horror film for several years after hearing noises in his attic. He kept the film secret from his friends and family, just in case it didn't work out.

Instead of writing a script, Peli focused on setting up his house with lighting and cameras and figuring out the technical aspects of filming. He held an open casting call, hiring unknown actors, and shot scenes using a handheld video camera. The film's

CHLOÉ ZHAO

Director Chloé Zhao has made her mark in independent films. Born in China, Zhao attended New York University's Tisch School of the Arts, where she studied under esteemed director Spike Lee. She began her career making short films. Her second short film, *Daughters*, received acclaim at several film festivals.

In 2015, Zhao wrote, directed, produced, and edited her first feature film, *Songs My Brothers Taught Me*. The film was shot on South Dakota's Pine Ridge Indian Reservation and premiered at Sundance Film Festival. Zhao's 2017 western drama *The Rider* also received critical acclaim.

In 2020, Zhao released the film *Nomadland*. It follows a widow who leaves her life behind after losing everything in an economic crash, traveling around the country in her van looking for work. The film won the Academy Award for Best Picture. Zhao won the Academy Award for Best Director, making her the second woman and first woman of color to do so. *Nomadland* also won Film Independent Spirit Awards for Best Movie, Best Director, and Best Editing. In 2021, Zhao shifted gears, directing and cowriting the screenplay for *Eternals*, a big-budget Marvel Studios superhero film.

In 2023, Chloé Zhao served as honorary co-chair of the 38th Film Independent Spirit Awards.

low-budget, home-video style lent itself to the story, which involved a character setting up a video camera to capture the demon-like presence lurking in the house. Most of the film was shot in just seven days.[9] *Paranormal Activity* became a smash hit that terrified audiences with its realism, launching a successful horror film franchise.

CREATIVE CONCEPTS

Indie films often allow directors to be more creative with content and scope than large studio movies do. This is because indie directors are not working under the control of a larger studio. Richard Linklater, for example, is known for making realistic, personal films on a low budget. His 1990 breakout film *Slacker* cost $23,000.[10] It was supported by a regional grant through the National Endowment for the Arts. The film became a cult classic, inspiring other filmmakers such as Kevin Smith to make their own independent films.

One indie filmmaking milestone was Linklater's 2014 film *Boyhood*, which follows a boy named Mason through childhood and into young adulthood. The movie was shot during the span of 12 years, between 2002 and 2013, and shows the characters as they aged in real time. Linklater gave the actors an outline rather than a full script. Made on a budget of $4 million, *Boyhood* earned $48 million at the box office and was critically acclaimed.[11]

Independent films such as *Boyhood* sometimes manage to cast big-name actors, who often take pay cuts in order to play a role they are passionate about. For instance, Hollywood star Ethan Hawke took a significant pay cut to be in *Boyhood*. Patricia Arquette, who plays Mason's mom, said she paid more money to her babysitter and dogwalker than what she made on the film.

SHOOTING ON A SMARTPHONE

Another indie filmmaking milestone came in 2015 with Sean Baker's *Tangerine*. The filmmakers used three iPhone 5S smartphones to shoot the comedy-drama, which tells the story of a transgender sex worker in Hollywood. In a positive

The Steadicam Smoothee comes with a mount for an iPhone and tools for adjusting the angle of a shot. The makers of *Tangerine* practiced using the Steadicam before shooting the film.

review, Lisa Mullen of the British Film Institute described the film as "guerilla-shot," referring to its street-style, nontraditional production.[12]

Knowledge about filmmaking basics is helpful for all moviemakers, no matter the scope of their projects. Although smartphones make filmmaking more accessible, the basics of filmmaking still apply. Filmmakers who want to create a professional film on a smartphone should be familiar with the filmmaking process and the phone's settings. For instance, to adjust the manual settings on a smartphone or camera, a filmmaker must understand terms such as frame rate and aperture. Some people invest in gear such as lenses or a smartphone gimbal, which keeps a camera level and steady.

The makers of *Tangerine* used the Filmic Pro video app, which allowed them to manually adjust the focus and exposure of the shots. The app also offered advanced compression so that the files were smaller, making it easier to store more footage. Each night, the filmmakers downloaded the files to a MacBook Pro. Later, they converted the files into larger sizes.

The filmmakers found a stabilizer, which is a type of camera mount, essential for making the film look professional. They used

FILMMAKING OVER ZOOM

Sometimes challenging circumstances lead to creativity in filmmaking. In 2020, Rob Savage used the format of a viral prank video he created to make *Host*, a feature-length indie horror film. The film was shot over Zoom while quarantine restrictions were in place during the COVID-19 pandemic, and the movie is set during a Zoom call. Savage directed the actors remotely, and the cast filmed themselves using phones taped to their laptops. The film was distributed by the streaming service Shudder.

a Steadicam Smoothee, a handheld support device that helps keep phone movements smooth and steady. Baker even used the Smoothee while riding a bike, turning the bike into a camera dolly. The team also used an anamorphic adapter lens fastened onto the phone to shoot widescreen footage and elevate the film's look. After experimenting in Final Cut Pro, Baker decided to saturate the film's color. A colorist did this using the Power Windows tool in the DaVinci Resolve software.

> **"I specifically wanted to shoot [the film *9 Rides*] with an iPhone because I wanted other filmmakers of color to know that it was possible to shoot a feature film with something that you have in your pocket, and also for it to be able to play at bigger film festivals and get distribution.[13]"**
>
> ***—Matthew Cherry, director***

CHAPTER **SEVEN**

POSTPRODUCTION OF INDEPENDENT MOVIES

Like professional filmmakers, indie filmmakers must do some editing after shooting film footage. This process involves trimming and cutting material, along with color correction and other adjustments. Popular software for video editing includes Avid Media Composer, DaVinci Resolve, Final Cut Pro, Lightworks, and Adobe Premiere Pro.

These programs are commonly used for editing footage, performing color correction, and adding visual effects and sound. Some basic editing programs are free, including iMovie, OpenShot, and CapCut. Filmmakers can use the Adobe After Effects software to create special effects, along with various animation techniques.

MARKETING INDEPENDENT FILMS

Marketing is essential if filmmakers want their movies to be seen. This is true whether the target audience is casual viewers on YouTube or a packed crowd at a public viewing. Although indie films operate on small budgets, filmmakers still need

When editing an indie film, filmmakers must consider color levels, sound, filters, transitions, and more. Sometimes indie directors or writers handle the editing process themselves.

On each project, I'd like to feel that there's something kind of insurmountable about it—some puzzle you have to solve or some element you have to crack or the whole thing doesn't work.[1]

—Richard Linklater, director

to get the word out about their movies. Today, social media platforms and internet resources are important assets in promoting any type of film, providing a wider reach than TV marketing.

One basic practice for marketing an indie film is creating an engaging trailer. Having good trailers is especially important for indie films because the marketing budget is lower and the stakes are higher. A good trailer hooks the viewer and gives them a sense of a film's tone, plot, conflicts, or any other interesting elements that will encourage audiences to watch the film.

Another way to promote a film is through social media. Platforms such as Facebook allow users to set a budget as part of an advertising campaign. With online advertising campaigns, filmmakers have the option to target audiences based on criteria such as gender, age, interests, and location.

Aside from the internet, filmmakers can find creative ways to market their films through other avenues. They can host in-person events to increase interest in their movies. They can also try to engage potential viewers through word-of-mouth. One way to do this is by approaching friends, family, bloggers, or influencers to talk about the film.

MAKING DISTRIBUTION PLANS

Some independent filmmakers work with a film distributor to get their films into theaters or on streaming platforms. Some distributors work with indie films specifically, rather than big-budget studio movies. One recommendation for filmmakers is to search for distributors that have worked with similar films or genres in the past.

Usually, film distributors have their guidelines on their websites. Some accept unsolicited film submissions, but most require submissions to come through a sales agent. This person works to sell the rights of the film. Most sales agents typically have relationships with industry professionals and distributors.

For film distribution directly through VOD release, filmmakers can work with an aggregator. This type of company works to get movies distributed on VOD. Aggregators usually have relationships with various platforms and sometimes take on the role of encoding, packaging, and delivering the film file. They may charge a fee along with a percentage of sales. Examples of aggregators include Filmhub, Bitmax, and Quiver.

A HORROR HIT

One of the most famous sleeper hits in indie movie history is the 1999 horror film *The Blair Witch Project*. It was written, directed, and edited by Daniel Myrick and Eduardo Sánchez. The story follows three film students who disappear after entering the woods to investigate a local legend. *The Blair Witch Project* premiered at Sundance Film Festival, where Artisan Entertainment bought the film. It earned more than $248 million at the box office and was influential in the horror genre.[2]

Some indie film distributors have become well known. For example, Barry Jenkins's 2016 film *Moonlight* was distributed by the successful indie studio A24.

Some film distribution deals happen before a movie is finished. However, if the film doesn't get completed, filmmakers may need to repay some money to the distributor. Although it can be difficult to find an agent without having industry connections, indie filmmakers can research agents or network at film festivals and other events. Having a strong social media presence can also help filmmakers secure distributors and agents.

Other indie filmmakers may release their film through a free platform, such as YouTube. Or they may distribute through the pay-per-view model, which includes theatrical releases or VOD. Another option is a subscription-based service, such as Netflix. There is also the ownership model, such as when people purchase DVDs.

The best distribution strategy for a film depends on the film's target audience. Filmmakers should think carefully about how their audience is going to view the movie. For instance, a filmmaker may choose to target their film as an exclusive, limited-time release at a drive-in theater, without offering a streaming option. Marketing efforts will focus on creating interest and excitement around the viewer experience of watching the film. This will leave audiences feeling like they don't want to miss seeing the film. One film that had a limited release was Greta Gerwig's 2017 film *Lady Bird*. It was originally shown at just four theaters in Los Angeles and New York City.[3] Later, it expanded to more theaters.

USING DATA

Knowing about digital data can be helpful to filmmakers when marketing their movies. Metadata is data that describes or gives meaning to other data. Within the source code on a webpage, metadata includes a page's title, description, and image. Search engines and sites use the metadata from a webpage to help index and share the page. Using proper metadata for a film can be a determining factor in connecting relevant audiences to a film. It can help the movie show up in search engine results, leading more people to a website, trailer, social media profile, or blog.

FILM FESTIVALS

Some filmmakers decide to show their movies at film festivals, which offer the opportunity to get films in front of an audience and potentially win awards and recognition. Film festivals of all sizes and genres take place around the world. Some are local festivals, while others are global. Major festivals include the Berlin International Film Festival in Germany,

Cannes Film Festival in France, Venice Film Festival in Italy, Sundance Film Festival in Utah, and Toronto International Film Festival in Canada.

Festivals can also be the launchpad for a distribution deal, depending on what industry professionals are present or how a film is reviewed. For instance, in 2020, Andy Samberg's comedy *Palm Springs* broke Sundance's record for the largest distribution deal ever. Hulu and independent distributor Neon purchased the film for $17.5 million.[4] It was later distributed through Hulu's streaming platform and in select theaters.

The following year, another streaming platform made a big move. Apple purchased Sian Heder's family drama *CODA* for approximately $25 million after the film premiered at Sundance.[5] Released through Apple TV+, the film became the first movie released through a streaming service to win an Academy Award for Best Picture.

"Festival programmers are always looking for things that stand out. So, if your film has a unique angle, be sure to point it out. . . . We're always looking for something that will differentiate the film beyond just the film itself.[6]"

—Drea Clark, film festival programmer

Many film festivals require films to premiere at the festival. That means filmmakers must be mindful of which film festivals they enter, as they have only one chance to debut their film. The internet is a helpful tool for researching film festivals and their guidelines. For example, some festivals require submitted films to have a sales agent, while others require all movies to have subtitles.

FILM MARKETS

Film markets can be another good opportunity for indie filmmakers. These trade shows give filmmakers a chance to present their films directly to distributors. Many different producers, distributors, and sales agents attend film markets. The distributor's employees at the market are known as acquisition executives. Some film markets take place at the same time as film festivals.

Major markets are held all over the world. This includes the Marché Du Film at the Cannes Film Festival, the American Film Market in California, the European Film Market at the Berlin International Film Festival, and the Asian Contents & Film Market at the Busan International Film Festival in South Korea.

The Sundance Film Festival features film screenings, panels, and awards ceremonies. It is one of the largest indie film festivals in the world.

At film markets such as the Marché Du Film, filmmakers can network with producers, distributors, and agents. They can also attend events and screenings.

Many different types of deals are made at film markets, even for films that are still in the development stage. At the markets, filmmakers have the opportunity to make appointments with distributors and pitch their movies. During this kind of meeting, the filmmaker usually gives a one-minute verbal pitch that explains why their film would be a good investment for the distributor. Distributors are often very short on time, so filmmakers should remember to provide them with an online media kit for their films. A good online media kit usually includes a trailer, clips, and a one-page breakdown of the film.

MAKING IT WORK

Indie filmmakers also have the option to distribute their movies themselves. They can release the film through theaters, but doing so is costly and requires paying for expenses such as ads. In the industry, renting a theater is known as "four-walling" the film. This is because the filmmaker is having the movie seen physically between four walls.

Filmmakers can also get TV or VOD deals. Some streaming services allow for independent application without a sales agent, but they may have other requirements. Crowdfunding and subscription services such as Patreon can help fund projects and keep audiences engaged.

Today, filmmakers have many options for getting their movies in front of audiences. The distribution process requires creativity, time, and money. It is important that filmmakers understand their audience and the objective of their films. Not every filmmaker is out to make a blockbuster, but every film can help raise awareness of a filmmaker's work and build up their credibility

FORMATTING A FILM

The film industry has certain standards for formatting a film. Today, most movies are made into digital files. Most theaters accept digital files in .mp4 format or .mov format. High-quality encoding allows the movie and its audio to be streamed online. Filmmakers also consider the aspect ratio of their film, which is the ratio of the image's width to its height. Films shown in theaters commonly have aspect ratios of 1.85:1 or 2.39:1. The aspect ratio of 16:9 is also used in filmmaking, while other ratios are used on various online platforms.[7]

1912
STATE
WE WILL BE BACK
AFTER A BRIEF
INTERMISSION
CONCERTS & EVENTS
NOW PLAYING

THE FUTURE OF MOVIES

Over the years, the film industry has continued to evolve. Today's filmmakers must navigate advances in technology, the impact of streaming services, and debates over AI. In recent years, labor disputes and calls for more diversity both on-screen and behind the camera have contributed to the changing film landscape.

The industry continues to reckon with big changes to the century-old Hollywood cinema model. In 2023, Terry Gross of National Public Radio (NPR) asked, "Is the industry collapsing or just reshaping? And what does this mean for viewers and for the future of entertainment?"[1] The answers remain to be seen.

After the early years of the COVID-19 pandemic, the film industry was still feeling the effects. In March 2023, box-office sales were still down about 35 percent from where they were pre-pandemic.[2] Some small theaters were forced to close due to the loss in business and the challenges of competing with streaming services and large theater chains. The top box-office movies continued to be familiar

The COVID-19 pandemic forced many large movie theater chains to temporarily close. But small movie theaters were hit even harder. A 2023 study found that more than 2,000 US movie theaters closed permanently during the height of the pandemic.

INTERACTIVE FILMS

Interactive films offer a new way to experience movies. Several well-received interactive films have been released in recent years, made possible with advances in technology and the proliferation of streaming services. Interactive films often allow the audience to use their remotes or touch screens to make choices that change the story. For example, Netflix's 2018 movie *Black Mirror: Bandersnatch* allows viewers to make decisions that lead to different plot points and endings.

big-budget franchises, with superhero films, horror films, and family films drawing audiences to theaters. In 2022, all ten of the top-grossing movies at the box office were sequels, prequels, or reboots, including installments from *Top Gun*, *Avatar*, *Jurassic Park*, *Doctor Strange*, and *Minions*.[3] Increasingly, genres such as dramas, comedies, and romantic comedies were releasing directly to streaming.

It was unknown if box-office numbers would continue to bounce back, but most industry experts agreed that audiences were unlikely to return to theaters in the same numbers as in the past. Some movie theater chains, such as AMC, have experimented with dynamic pricing models, which offer different seats at different prices. Offering lower-priced seats could attract more people to theaters.

STREAMING SERVICES

Many filmmakers and filmgoers have embraced the benefits of streaming. Films that would normally have limited theatrical releases are now available to much wider audiences via streaming. In recent years, more original films have been produced per year

A Netflix account is for people who live in the same location

Everyone who lives at your primary location can use Netflix when they're on the go or traveling.

If this is your account, we'll help you set your primary location on the next screen.

Continue

Many Netflix users share accounts with people outside of their households. But Netflix began cracking down on password sharing, limiting account access by household.

than ever before. However, some industry experts predict that the influx of streaming content will soon settle down. They say this is because streaming services will merge over time, causing companies to spend less money creating content in an effort to entice new subscribers.

Today, streaming services continue to upend the traditional movie industry. Several streaming services are owned by huge media conglomerates, such as Disney. It owns Pixar, Marvel, and Lucasfilm, offering films from these companies on the platform Disney+. For some streaming services, such as Amazon, streaming is just one aspect of their sprawling company. This makes their business stakes much different from those of traditional Hollywood studios of the past. Streaming services can also make big

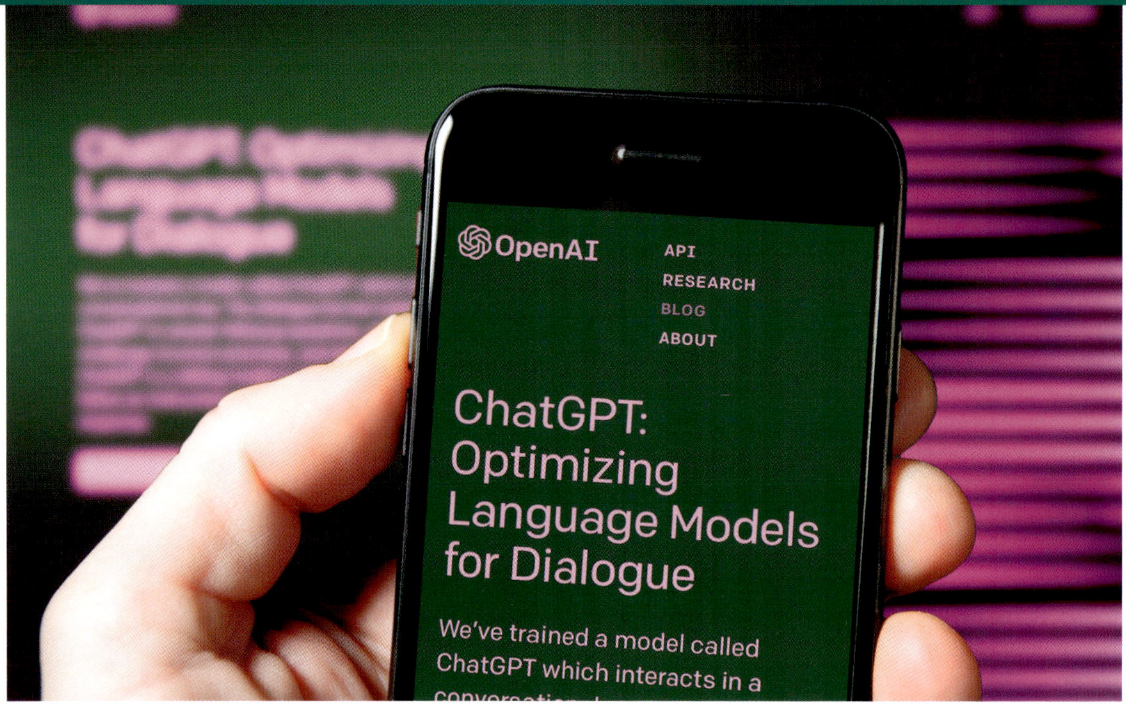

ChatGPT was launched by OpenAI, an AI research company. The tool can quickly generate film scripts, loglines, and pitches. Critics worry that this technology will take jobs away from people in the film industry.

waves by increasing prices for their subscribers. In 2023, for example, Netflix raised the price of its basic subscription plan from $9.99 a month to $11.99 a month. Its ad-free plan increased from $19.99 to $22.99.[4]

ARTIFICIAL INTELLIGENCE

One increasingly hot topic in filmmaking and other industries is AI. AI technology could potentially be used for many parts of the filmmaking process that are normally performed by humans. For instance, AI could assist with casting, create storyboards and special effects, and perform audience research. It could even be used to make decisions about film distribution. This could entice producers and studios who want to save time and money.

AI is already being used in various ways, including in postproduction video editing. Algorithms can pick out the best shots and assist with effects, sharpening, and color grading. Adobe's Firefly AI model is an example of this. Champions of AI say that it could give filmmakers more time and ways to collaborate remotely with each other. They believe AI should be viewed as a tool to enhance what humans are doing, rather than as a threat. For instance, AI could help filmmakers be more efficient with their budgets. It could make filmmaking accessible to more people, giving them more time to dive into the creative process.

> **"AI is already earning comparisons to the agricultural revolution, industrial revolution, and internet revolution. It is moving fast and gathering speed. The most profound effects for Hollywood. . . have probably not yet been imagined.[5]"**
>
> ***—David Smith,* the Guardian*, 2023***

However, the use of AI also raises ethical concerns. Many people point out the risk of the machines eventually replacing human talent and creativity. In 2023, the AI chatbot tool ChatGPT made headlines with its ability to generate humanlike text. It could write essays, hold conversations, and even take exams. While some people may be comfortable with using AI to help develop movie ideas, others are concerned about the possibility of AI writing entire movie scripts or making revisions. One concern with using AI for script writing is the kinds of stories it would produce. Since AI uses information that it receives to formulate its answers, it only represents the set of people who are programming it. This could lead to a lack in diversity and representation in film.

AI has already been used for deepfakes and voice replication. Because of this, some groups are calling for more regulation of the technology. The National Association of Voice Actors has raised concerns about AI taking work away from real people if their voices are used without their permission. Actors such as Keanu Reeves have even built stipulations into their contracts that ban studios from using AI on their performances without their consent. Although the full scope of AI in film is impossible to foresee, its use is likely to have long-lasting social and economic effects.

LABOR DISPUTES

Actors, writers, and other workers in Hollywood continue to grapple with what AI, streaming, and other changing technologies mean for their jobs and pay. These issues were at the forefront of Hollywood labor disputes between film studios and artists that began in May 2023. The Writers Guild of America (WGA) went on strike against the

Many TV and film casts reunited to participate in the 2023 SAG-AFTRA strike. Several members of the *Breaking Bad* cast were among the strikers.

SAG·AFTRA
ON
STRIKE!
SAG·AFTRA
ON
STRIKE!
SAG·AFTRA
ON
STRIKE!

The film *Everything Everywhere All at Once* features many Asian and Asian American cast and crew members. In 2023, the film won seven Academy Awards, including Best Actress and Best Picture.

Alliance of Motion Picture and Television Producers (AMPTP). In July 2023, the US actors' union, SAG-AFTRA, joined the WGA by going on strike. The union had 160,000 members.[6]

The artists called for various protections and the regulation of AI technologies, as well as new terms for residuals from streaming services. Residuals are payments made to cast and crew members for reruns, airings, streaming, or other uses after a film's or show's initial release. Many people who work on films earn little to no residuals when their shows or movies are played on streaming services. Actor Aaron Paul, who starred in the hit TV series *Breaking Bad*, told reporters that he doesn't "get a piece from Netflix" on the show. "Shows live forever on these streamers and it goes through waves," he said. "I think a lot of these streamers . . . know they have been getting away with not paying people just fair wage."[7]

Actress Hayley Atwell also called out studios and streaming companies for their exploitation of industry workers. "That's unacceptable when you've got heads of streaming services and studios making profits of hundreds of millions of dollars," she said.[8] The strikes gained public support from other entertainment unions, including the Directors Guild of America and the International Alliance of Theatrical Stage Employees. The strikes halted Hollywood production, meaning only projects without writers and actors, such as reality TV, could continue shooting.

The WGA strike ended in September 2023, with the WGA and studio heads reaching a tentative agreement. At 148 days, it was the second-longest strike in Hollywood history.[9] The parties were able to come to terms on several key points, such as the use of AI in the creative process, staffing requirements, and streaming residuals. The agreement also included terms that allowed writers to choose when to use AI and said that a writer's work cannot be used to train AI. The SAG-AFTRA strike

MAKING THE MULTIVERSE

The directing duo Dan Kwan and Daniel Scheinert became industry sensations with their 2022 film *Everything Everywhere All at Once*, starring Michelle Yeoh. The low-budget independent film was distributed by A24. It won seven Academy Awards, including Best Picture and Best Film Editing, and raked in more than $143 million at the box office.[10] The movie's plot centered on Yeoh's character traveling through multiple universes, which required extensive visual effects. The film's effects team worked remotely throughout the pandemic. For a year and half, the artists used Adobe After Effects, Cinema 4D animation and modeling software, and other programs to create the effects. The film broke barriers with its representation of Asian and Asian American actors and filmmakers.

In 2015, the hashtag #OscarsSoWhite took over social media. Writer and activist April Reign coined the term after the year's all-white acting Academy Awards nominees were announced. The phrase spread, sparking discussions about inclusivity and representation in Hollywood. However, industry analysts continued to call out the same issues in 2023, pointing out that no Black director had ever won an Academy Award, and no Black woman had ever received a nomination for directing. The same issues of underrepresentation were reflected in various industry organizations and in the basic power structures of Hollywood, influencing which films were greenlit, funded, and nominated for awards.

ended in November 2023. The union's agreement with studio heads included payment increases, protections against AI, and a streaming participation bonus.

LIMITLESS STORIES

In recent years, people have been calling for more diversity and representation both on-screen and behind the camera. Studies show that Hollywood still has a lot of work to do. Diversity in race, ethnicity, and gender among movie actors, directors, and writers in theatrical releases has been on the rise for several years.

But a 2023 University of California, Los Angeles (UCLA) report found that those areas had fallen slightly. For example, in 2019, people of color made up about 28 percent of lead roles in theatrical films. In 2022, that number dropped to about 22 percent.[11] The report also found that movies released on streaming services were more diverse than theatrical releases.

Women and people of color continue to make strides in the industry, but they remain underrepresented in cinema. The 2023 UCLA report found that women directed only 15 percent of theatrical films in 2022.[12] People with disabilities were also found to be underrepresented. Another 2023 study by the Latino Donor Collaborative found that the representation of Latino people in TV and film was declining. This caused audiences to shift away from traditional viewing to platforms such as YouTube and TikTok, which featured more Latino creators. The data inspired many people to urge Hollywood to invest in films that reflect the diversity of its audience.

As filmmakers look to the future, the industry seems full of possibilities for new creative visions and forms of storytelling. Studios, producers, and filmmakers are working to navigate changes in how movies are made and distributed. However, change in cinema is nothing new. From its beginnings in silent movies to today's world of experimentation, accessibility, and film on demand, the film industry has continued to grow.

With no set formula for success, the door remains open for new ideas and innovation. Filmmakers continue to explore different ways to finance, shoot, edit, and distribute movies. No matter the scope or size of their films, filmmakers who can carry out their visions, tell engaging stories, adapt their approaches, and tap into audiences have the potential for success.

> **"We have to find new ways to work without permission, new ways to turn corners and go through doors that are closed off to us to create our own audiences and our own material independently.[13]"**
>
> ***—Ava DuVernay, director***

ESSENTIAL **FACTS**

MAKING MOVIES PROFESSIONALLY

- The first step in making a professional movie is developing a concept or idea. A screenwriter or filmmaker writes a script based on the concept. They pitch it to producers or studios.
- Once a film project is given the green light, preproduction begins. This involves finalizing a budget, setting a schedule, scouting locations, hiring cast and crew members, and creating costumes and props.
- The next stage is production, which involves shooting the film. After filming wraps, postproduction begins. The film team works on editing, color adjustments, visual effects, and other tasks.
- Distributors help market the film with the aim of showing it to as many people as possible. Big-budget studio films often have a large portion of their budget dedicated to marketing.

MAKING MOVIES INDEPENDENTLY

- The first step in making an independent film is to develop a concept. The screenplay, schedule, and budget are created. Indie films typically have smaller budgets and crews compared with major productions. Filmmakers may fund the project themselves or raise money through crowdfunding.
- The production process begins. The basics of filmmaking apply to small-budget indie films. Filmmakers may take on multiple roles during production.
- After production wraps, indie filmmakers use software programs and apps to edit their film footage. They also prepare marketing materials such as trailers.
- Independent filmmakers distribute their films through the internet, film festivals, or other venues. Sometimes they make a deal with a distributor for a wider release of the film.

QUOTE

"Each project comes with its own set of challenges. . . . once I feel [that a film] is important enough to make, then it is your passion, your drive, and your determination that take it to the next level."

—*Kathryn Bigelow, director*

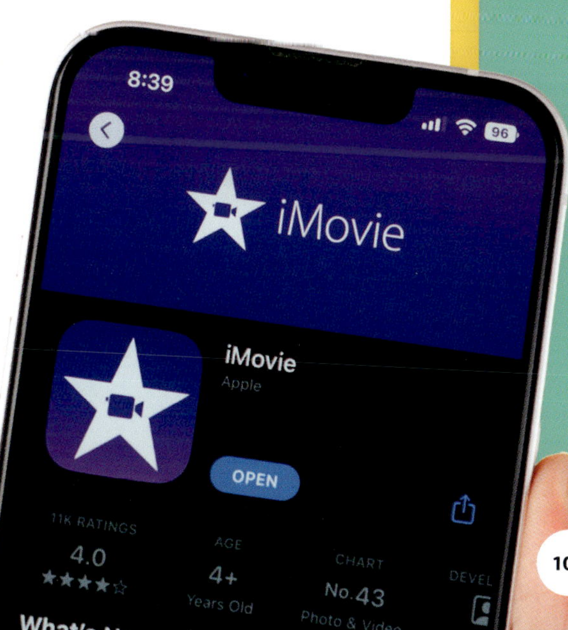

GLOSSARY

camera dolly
A cart on wheels that a camera is mounted on to create a smooth shot.

cinematography
Motion picture photography.

computer-generated imagery (CGI)
Technology that uses computer graphics to make visual content.

cult classic
A film that is popular among a small but loyal group.

deepfake
A form of media that has been digitally altered to realistically look or sound like another person.

film theory
The study of film, including film analysis and criticism.

franchise
A series of films, as well as other associated media, that share a setting, a story, or characters.

gross
To earn income.

improvise
To act without planning ahead of time.

public domain
Not subject to copyright.

saturation
The intensity of color in an image.

sleeper hit
A film that has gradual, unexpected success.

subvert
To overturn expectations or norms.

ADDITIONAL RESOURCES

SELECTED BIBLIOGRAPHY

Heckmann, Chris. "The History of Film Timeline–All Eras of Film History Explained." *StudioBinder*, 1 Jan. 2023, studiobinder.com. Accessed 17 Jan. 2024.

"How to Make a Movie: Everything You Need to Know." *Nashville Film Institute*, n.d., nfi.edu. Accessed 16 Oct. 2023.

Lincoln, Kevin. "How to Make a Movie on Your Smartphone." *Vulture*, 13 Nov. 2018, vulture.com. Accessed 4 Aug. 2023.

FURTHER READINGS

McKinney, Donna B. *The Actor Encyclopedia*. Abdo, 2024.

Murray, Laura K. *The Movie Encyclopedia*. Abdo, 2024.

ONLINE RESOURCES

To learn more about making movies, please visit **abdobooklinks.com** or scan this QR code. These links are routinely monitored and updated to provide the most current information available.

MORE INFORMATION

For more information on this subject, contact or visit the following organizations:

Academy of Motion Picture Arts and Sciences
Academy Headquarters
8949 Wilshire Blvd.
Beverly Hills, CA 90211
oscars.org
The Academy of Motion Picture Arts and Sciences has more than 10,000 members in the film industry. The academy hosts the Academy Awards, or Oscars, each year.

American Film Institute (AFI)
2021 North Western Ave.
Los Angeles, CA 90027
afi.com
The American Film Institute (AFI) is a nonprofit focused on celebrating film. AFI hosts education initiatives, film festivals, clubs, awards, resources, and historical archives.

Sundance Institute
1500 Kearns Blvd., Ste. B110
Park City, UT 84060
sundance.org
The Sundance Institute is a nonprofit dedicated to independent storytelling. The institute hosts Utah's Sundance Film Festival, one of the most famous film festivals in North America.

SOURCE NOTES

CHAPTER 1. MAKING A MOVIE

1. Steve Chagollan. "Passion Player." *Directors Guild of America Quarterly*, n.d., dga.org. Accessed 7 Dec. 2023.
2. Kevin Lincoln. "How to Make a Movie on Your Smartphone." *Vulture*, 13 Nov. 2018, vulture.com. Accessed 7 Dec. 2023.

CHAPTER 2. THE HISTORY OF MOVIES

1. Kyle DeGuzman. "The Lumière Brothers—Pioneers of the Silver Screen." *StudioBinder*, 12 Nov. 2023, studiobinder.com. Accessed 7 Dec. 2023.
2. "*The Great Train Robbery*." *AFI Catalog of Feature Films*, n.d., aficatalog.afi.com. Accessed 7 Dec. 2023.
3. "Understanding Media and Culture: An Introduction to Mass Communication." *University of Minnesota Libraries Publishing*, n.d., open.lib.umn.edu. Accessed 7 Dec. 2023.
4. "Understanding Media and Culture."
5. Amber Paranick. "Alice Guy-Blaché: Cinema's First Woman Director in Newspapers." *Library of Congress Blogs*, 26 Jan. 2022, blogs.loc.gov. Accessed 7 Dec. 2023.
6. "Understanding Media and Culture."
7. "13 Essential Films to Watch in Honor of Sidney Poitier." *A.frame*, n.d., aframe.oscars.org. Accessed 7 Dec. 2023.
8. K. Austin Collins. "Why Olivia de Havilland Took Jack Warner to Court—and Won." *Vanity Fair*, 28 July 2020, vanityfair.com. Accessed 7 Dec. 2023.
9. Richard Fink, Timea, Jack Deegan, and Callum Jones. "The Most Expensive Movies Ever Made." *MovieWeb*, 8 Nov. 2023, movieweb.com. Accessed 7 Dec. 2023.
10. Pamela McClintock. "2021 Global Box Office Down 50 Percent from Pre-Pandemic Times: MPA Report." *Hollywood Reporter*, 14 Mar. 2022, hollywoodreporter.com. Accessed 7 Dec. 2023.
11. Rebecca Rubin. "Global Box Office Hits New Record in 2019 with $42.5 Billion." *Variety*, 10 Jan. 2020, variety.com. Accessed 7 Dec. 2023.
12. Patrick Frater. "Global Box Office Notched 27% Gain in 2022 to Hit $26 Billion Total, Research Shows." *Variety*, 5 Jan. 2023, variety.com. Accessed 7 Dec. 2023.
13. Lilia Luciano and Analisa Novak. "Huge Changes Underway in Film Industry as It Reckons with Streaming, Pandemic Impact." *CBS News*, 10 Mar. 2023, cbsnews.com. Accessed 7 Dec. 2023.

CHAPTER 3. PREPRODUCTION OF PROFESSIONAL MOVIES

1. Ari Eisner. "The Movie Logline: What It Is and How to Write One (with Examples)." *CareersinFilm*, 20 June 2023, careersinfilm.com. Accessed 7 Dec. 2023.
2. Eisner, "The Movie Logline."
3. Richard Fink, Timea, Jack Deegan, and Callum Jones. "The Most Expensive Movies Ever Made." *MovieWeb*, 8 Nov. 2023, movieweb.com. Accessed 7 Dec. 2023.
4. Mekado Murphy. "Waiting for the Credits to End? Movies Are Naming More Names." *New York Times*, 26 Mar. 2017, nytimes.com. Accessed 8 Dec. 2023.
5. Ana Bogdan. "Ellen Kuras: 'I've Always Worked in My Mind's Eye.'" *Talks*, n.d., the-talks.com. Accessed 8 Dec. 2023.

CHAPTER 4. PRODUCTION OF PROFESSIONAL MOVIES

1. Margaret Kurniawan and Hiroshi Hara. "A Guide to Principal Photography in Film." *Adobe*, n.d., adobe.com. Accessed 8 Dec. 2023.

2. Sarah Ball. "What You Should Know about Roger Deakins." *Vanity Fair*, 25 Feb. 2014, vanityfair.com. Accessed 8 Dec. 2023.

3. "Roger Deakins: Awards." *IMDb*, n.d., imbd.com. Accessed 8 Dec. 2023.

4. Susan Stamberg. "Behind This Exuberant Dance Number? Planning, Precision and Practice." *NPR*, 21 Feb. 2017, npr.org. Accessed 8 Dec. 2023.

5. Valerie Gladstone. "DANCE; When Battle and Ballet Become Synonymous." *New York Times*, 3 Dec. 2000, nytimes.com. Accessed 8 Dec. 2023.

6. Vincent LoBrutto. *Principal Photography: Interviews with Feature Film Cinematographers*. Praeger, 1999. 102.

7. Phil de Semlyen, Helen O'Hara, Matthew Singer, and James Balmont. "The 18 Most Mind-Blowing Stunts in Movie History." *Time Out*, 23 Jan. 2023, timeout.com. Accessed 8 Dec. 2023.

8. Jay Holben, Steven Bernstein, and Cody Liesinger. "Assemble and Refine Footage with Post-Production." *Adobe*, n.d., adobe.com. Accessed 8 Dec. 2023.

CHAPTER 5. DISTRIBUTION OF PROFESSIONAL MOVIES

1. Philip Paquette. "Producer's Guide: Film Distributors." *Wrapbook*, 30 Sept. 2020, wrapbook.com. Accessed 8 Dec. 2023.

2. Rex Provost. "What Is Film Distribution—The Ultimate Guide for Filmmakers." *StudioBinder*, 2 July 2023, studiobinder.com. Accessed 8 Dec. 2023.

3. Nick Zieminksi. "'All Quiet on the Western Front' Wins Oscar for Best International Film." *Reuters*, 12 Mar. 2023, reuters.com. Accessed 8 Dec. 2023.

4. Elaine Roberts. "How to Market Your Movie." *Backstage*, 20 Nov. 2023, backstage.com. Accessed 8 Dec. 2023.

5. "Movie Taglines: 116 Taglines You Should Know." *Nashville Film Institute*, n.d., nfi.edu. Accessed 8 Dec. 2023.

6. Rebecca Rubin. "Inside 'Barbie's' Pink Publicity Machine: How Warner Bros. Pulled Off the Marketing Campaign of the Year." *Variety*, 23 July 2023, variety.com. Accessed 8 Dec. 2023.

7. Rubin, "Inside 'Barbie's' Pink Publicity Machine."

8. Eva Rothenberg. "'Barbie' Makes History with $1 Billion at the Box Office." *CNN*, 6 Aug. 2023, cnn.com. Accessed 8 Dec. 2023.

9. Marcos Franco. "The 10 Most Lucrative Movie Merchandise Franchises." *IndieWire*, 6 Aug. 2023, indiewire.com. Accessed 8 Dec. 2023.

10. "*Avengers: Endgame*." *Box Office Mojo*, n.d., boxofficemojo.com. Accessed 8 Dec. 2023.

11. Aidan Kelley. "'Avengers: Endgame' Budget Breakdown: Dissecting the Infinity Saga's Record-Breaking Finale." *Collider*, 8 July 2023, collider.com. Accessed 8 Dec. 2023.

12. Tom Brueggemann. "Confused about When You Can Watch Movies at Home? Get Used to It." *IndieWire*, 3 Apr. 2023, indiewire.com. Accessed 8 Dec. 2023.

CHAPTER 6. DEVELOPING AND PRODUCING INDEPENDENT MOVIES

1. Carli Montague. "George Clooney Accepted a $3 Salary for an Oscar-Nominated Film." *Showbiz Cheat Sheet*, 7 Dec. 2020, cheatsheet.com. Accessed 8 Dec. 2023.
2. Chris Cullari. "The Full Budget and Income Breakdown of *Paranormal Activity*." *Wrapbook*, 15 Mar. 2023, wrapbook.com. Accessed 8 Dec. 2023.
3. Stephen Barker. "The 10 Highest-Grossing Independent Films of All Time." *Screen Rant*, 17 Oct. 2020, screenrant.com. Accessed 8 Dec. 2023.
4. Daniel Bukszpan. "The 15 Most Profitable Movies of All Time." *CNBC*, 29 Jan. 2014, cnbc.com. Accessed 8 Dec. 2023.
5. Angela Watercutter. "The First Kickstarter Film to Win an Oscar Takes Home Crowdsourced Gold." *Wired*, 25 Feb. 2023, wired.com. Accessed 8 Dec. 2023.
6. Marlow Stern. "Sofia Coppola Discusses 'Lost in Translation' on Its 10th Anniversary." *Daily Beast*, 11 July 2017, thedailybeast.com. Accessed 8 Dec. 2023.
7. Nathan Hilgartner. "The Full Budget and Income Breakdown of *Clerks*." *Wrapbook*, 22 Mar. 2023, wrapbook.com. Accessed 8 Dec. 2023.
8. Reid Goldberg. "How Kevin Smith Parlayed $27,575 into a Career Spanning Three Decades." *Collider*, 20 Mar. 2023, collider.com. Accessed 18 Dec. 2023.
9. Ethan Alter. "How 'Paranormal Activity' Became the Scariest, Most Successful DIY Horror Movie Ever." *Yahoo! Entertainment*, 12 Oct. 2022, yahoo.com. Accessed 8 Dec. 2023.
10. Teddy Wansink. "Realism on the Reel: The Cinematic Vision of Richard Linklater." *National Endowment for the Arts*, 29 Jan. 2019, arts.gov. Accessed 8 Dec. 2023.
11. Mark Hughes. "Richard Linklater and the Artistic Restraint of 'Boyhood.'" *Forbes*, 19 Feb. 2015, forbes.com. Accessed 8 Dec. 2023.
12. Lisa Mullen. "Film of the Week: *Tangerine*." *British Film Institute*, 18 Nov. 2016, bfi.org.uk. Accessed 8 Dec. 2023.
13. Kevin Lincoln. "How to Make a Movie on Your Smartphone." *Vulture*, 13 Nov. 2018, vulture.com. Accessed 8 Dec. 2023.

CHAPTER 7. POSTPRODUCTION OF INDEPENDENT MOVIES

1. Mark Hughes. "Richard Linklater and the Artistic Restraint of 'Boyhood.'" *Forbes*, 19 Feb. 2015, forbes.com. Accessed 8 Dec. 2023.
2. Anna Keizer. "The Full Budget and Income Breakdown of *The Blair Witch Project*." *Wrapbook*, 8 Mar. 2023, wrapbook.com. Accessed 8 Dec. 2023.
3. Brian Brooks. "Greta Gerwig's 'Lady Bird' Takes Year's Best Per Theater Average of $93K—Specialty Box Office." *Deadline*, 5 Nov. 2017, deadline.com. Accessed 8 Dec. 2023.
4. Matt Donnelly. "'Palm Springs' Breaks Sundance Record for Biggest Sale Ever—By 69 Cents." *Variety*, 27 Jan. 2020, variety.com. Accessed 8 Dec. 2023.
5. Chris Lindahl. "Apple's $25 Million 'CODA' Acquisition Smashes Sundance Sales Record." *IndieWire*, 30 Jan. 2021, indiewire.com. Accessed 8 Dec. 2023.
6. "8 Tips for Getting into Film Festivals, from a Sundance Programmer." *Musicbed*, n.d., musicbed.com. Accessed 18 Dec. 2023.
7. "The Definitive Guide to Aspect Ratio." *StudioBinder,* 12 Apr. 2020, studiobinder.com. Accessed 8 Dec. 2023.

CHAPTER 8. THE FUTURE OF MOVIES

1. Terry Gross. "Is the TV/Film Industry Collapsing, or Just Reshaping Itself for the Future?" *NPR*, 21 July 2023, npr.org. Accessed 8 Dec. 2023.

2. Lilia Luciano and Analisa Novak. "Huge Changes Underway in Film Industry as It Reckons with Streaming Pandemic Impact." *CBS News*, 10 Mar. 2023, cbsnews.com. Accessed 8 Dec. 2023.

3. Jordan Ruimy. "The 10 Highest Grossing Movies of 2022 Were All Sequels and Reboots." *World of Reel*, 31 Dec. 2022, worldofreel.com. Accessed 8 Dec. 2023.

4. David Pierce. "Streaming Services Keep Getting More Expensive: All the Latest Price Increases." *Verge*, 2 Nov. 2023, theverge.com. Accessed 8 Dec. 2023.

5. David Smith. "'Of Course It's Disturbing:' Will AI Change Hollywood Forever?" *Guardian*, 23 Mar. 2023, theguardian.com. Accessed 8 Dec. 2023.

6. Caitlin Huston. "Writers Guild, Directors Guild Send SAG-AFTRA Solidarity Messages as Its Strike Begins." *Hollywood Reporter*, 13 July 2023, hollywoodreporter.com. Accessed 8 Dec. 2023.

7. Kirsty Hatcher. "Aaron Paul Says It's 'Insane' He Doesn't 'Get a Piece' of 'Breaking Bad' Residuals from Netflix." *People*, 6 Sept. 2023, people.com. Accessed 8 Dec. 2023.

8. Samantha Chery, Avi Selk, and Janay Kingsberry. "What Actors Are Saying about the Strike on SAG Picket Lines." *Washington Post*, 27 July 2023, washingtonpost.com. Accessed 8 Dec. 2023.

9. Alissa Wilkinson and Emily Stewart. "The Hollywood Writers' Strike Is Over—and They Won Big." *Vox*, 28 Sept. 2023, vox.com. Accessed 8 Dec. 2023.

10. "*Everything Everywhere All at Once*." *Box Office Mojo*, n.d., boxofficemojo.com. Accessed 8 Dec. 2023.

11. Dr. Ana-Christina Ramón, Michael Tran, and Dr. Darnell Hunt. "Hollywood Diversity Report 2023." *UCLA College of Social Sciences*, n.d., socialsciences.ucla.edu. Accessed 8 Dec. 2023.

12. Ramón, et al., "Hollywood Diversity Report 2023."

13. Alanna Vagianos. "Ava DuVernay: Women Need to Find 'New Ways to Work without Permission.'" *HuffPost*, 7 Oct. 2016, huffpost.com. Accessed 8 Dec. 2023.

INDEX

ABOUT THE **AUTHOR**

LAURA K. MURRAY

Laura K. Murray has written more than 100 nonfiction books on subjects ranging from music and pop culture to history and science. She lives in Minnesota.